MORE THAN MONEY

Published by CelebrityPress™, Orlando, FL
A division of The Celebrity Branding Agency®

Celebrity Branding® is a registered trademark
Printed in the United States of America.

ISBN: 978-0-9829083-8-9
LCCN: 2010943530

This publication is designed to provide accurate and authoritative information with regard to the subject matter covered. It is sold with the understanding that the publisher is not engaged in rendering legal, accounting, or other professional advice. If legal advice or other expert assistance is required, the services of a competent professional should be sought. The opinions expressed by the authors in this book are not endorsed by CelebrityPress™ and are the sole responsibility of the author rendering the opinion.

Most CelebrityPress™ titles are available at special quantity discounts for bulk purchases for sales promotions, premiums, fundraising, and educational use. Special versions or book excerpts can also be created to fit specific needs.

For more information, please write:

CelebrityPress™,
520 N. Orlando Ave, #44,
Winter Park, FL 32789

or call 1.877.261.4930

Visit us online at www.**CelebrityPressPublishing**.com

MORE THAN MONEY

How to Leave a Lasting Legacy to Your Family

TABLE OF CONTENTS:

FOREWORD
BY ALEXIS NEELY, ESQ. 11

CHAPTER 1
WHO WILL IF YOU CAN'T?
BY ALEXIS NEELY, ESQ. 13

CHAPTER 2
PERSPECTIVE
BY MARTHA J. HARTNEY, ESQ. 23

CHAPTER 3
LESSONS LEARNED THE HARD WAY
BY RICHARD S. CARLYON, ESQ. 31

CHAPTER 4
HOW TO LEAVE A LEGACY THAT LASTS...
BY KRISTINA R. HAYMES, ESQ. 43

CHAPTER 5
IF ONLY THEY HAD KNOWN...
EVALUATING AN ESTATE FROM A PERSONAL PERSPECTIVE
BY KYRA FISCHBECK HOWELL, ESQ. 49

CHAPTER 6
LEGACY OF LOVE – PART I
THE VALUE OF EMOTIONAL ASSETS
BY GEMINI ADAMS...59

CHAPTER 7
LEGACY OF LOVE – PART II
GETTING TO GRIPS WITH GRIEF
BY GEMINI ADAMS...71

CHAPTER 8
LEGACY OF LOVE – PART III
LIFE CELEBRATION
BY GEMINI ADAMS...87

CHAPTER 9
**BELIEVE – THE LEGACY YOU LEAVE
LASTS FOREVER**
BY JUDY ROSS, ESQ...103

CHAPTER 10
PUT YOUR HOUSE IN ORDER
BY MEG OBENAUF, ESQ...113

CHAPTER 11
**THE RISE AND RUIN OF A
REAL ESTATE FORTUNE**
BY PETER SAHIN, ESQ...123

CHAPTER 12
ESTATE PLANNING: MAKE IT PERSONAL
BY CHRISTINE E. FAULKNER, ESQ..131

CHAPTER 13
'THAT WILL NEVER HAPPEN TO ME' – THE MYTH!
BY TERESA DE FORD, ESQ. 141

CHAPTER 14
LEGACY OF YOUR ACTIONS
BY R. DEDE SOTO, ESQ...149

CHAPTER 15
**ARRANGE TO TRANSFER YOUR ASSETS FOR
YOUR HEIRS SAKE**
BY ROWEL MANASAN, ESQ...163

CHAPTER 16
WISDOM IS THE LEGACY
BY MARTHA J. HARTNEY, ESQ...171

CHAPTER 17
LEAVE A LEGACY FOR YOUR FAMILY
BY GARY L. WINTER, ESQ..179

CHAPTER 18
CAN YOU REALLY DO WITHOUT MONEY?
BY ROBERT GALLIANO, ESQ...189

FOREWORD

This is a book about the meaning of life, why we are really here and what happens when you die.

...And it's written by lawyers.

Why are lawyers writing about esoteric subjects usually reserved for philosophers and theologists? Because lawyers are the ones who see what really happens, beyond all the theory and wonder.

Because it is these lawyers who get the 'up close and personal' view of the reality of it, and work with their clients on a daily basis to help leave a real, lasting, meaningful legacy; one that is about so much more than money.

At the end of your life, when your family doesn't know what to do or how to handle the logistics of illness and death, they call a lawyer.

Hopefully, they'll call your personal lawyer, the one you created a relationship with while you were living and well. If you didn't take the time and make the effort to establish such a relationship, they ask friends for a referral or turn to the internet in search of someone to guide them.

What your family has to deal with during this time of deep grief and stress is part of your legacy, ...a big part. And yet it is one we so often overlook as we get caught up in the day-to-day of living our lives in the 'here and now'.

When you really start to pay attention to the legacy you'll leave at the end of your life, your 'here and now' changes. It's time for you to see what really matters when it comes to legacy.

Before we get into the book, let's talk a bit about what legacy really means.

Legacy has two definitions:

1. Money or property bequeathed to another by will.
2. Something handed down from an ancestor or a predecessor or from the past.

Throughout this book, the legacy we'll be talking about is the type that goes beyond money or property bequeathed in your will, although we will certainly touch on that.

What we will be focusing on is the legacy of you. Your values, your insights, your stories and your experience. What are you handing down to our future generations? Are you leaving this legacy consciously or by default? And how can a book by a bunch of lawyers help you create a real, lasting, meaningful legacy that goes far beyond your will?

Read on to find out … these are no ordinary lawyers and after reading what they have to say about legacy, your life will be no ordinary life.

CHAPTER 1

WHO WILL IF YOU CAN'T?

BY ALEXIS NEELY, ESQ.

Do you remember the first airplane trip you took after the birth of your children? I sure do. It was the first time I consciously thought of the legacy I wanted to leave my children.

Up until then, I had thought a lot about where I wanted them to go to school, who would look after them while I was at work, and what to do for their birthday celebrations, but I hadn't given a whole lot of thought to what I wanted to leave with them after I was gone.

Getting on that plane, *it hit me like a hard slap across the face – I might not be there to raise them!*

It was then that I began to realize … I had not given near enough thought to what would happen to my children if something happened to me. How would they be raised? And by who? Would they know how much I loved them? Or would they end up scarred for life because I hadn't written the love letters I had intended to write on each birthday? I hated myself for not having taken the time to do it before then.

And then the plane landed safely, I got to the hotel and promptly forgot about all my fears as I soaked in a quiet tub for the first time in ages. By the time I got home and got caught back up into the hustle of day-to-day life, I had forgotten all about writing those love letters once again.

It wasn't until I started my own law firm, and created my own Will and Trust in preparation for serving my clients, that I began to think about these issues again. When I did, I discovered that the typical planning parents do for their minor children is woefully inadequate.

As I began to think through the reality of naming guardians in a Will for my own children, I saw so clearly that a Will alone would never be enough to ensure my babies would be taken care of by the people I wanted, in the way I wanted, and never be taken into the arms of strangers.

I looked deeper into the planning parents were doing for their children, and found out that 69% of parents have never named guardians for their kids at all, and of the 31% who have, most had made at least one of 6 mistakes that would leave their kids at risk. (Wondering if you've made one of the 6 common mistakes most parents make when naming guardians for their kids? See http://www.KidsProtectionPlan.com where you can read about the 6 mistakes and name legal guardians for your children for free.)

I began to have conversations with parents who had named guardians for their children, thought they did the right thing by planning, and were walking around with a false sense of security thinking everything had been taken care of when in fact it was not. Not by a long shot. I knew I needed to do something about it.

So, I started with my own family. I decided I would create a legacy for my children that would be about far more than the money I was leaving them, and that would ensure they would always be raised by the people I wanted, in the way I wanted. But first I had to figure out what that was. How did I want my kids raised? …And by who?

I began an inquiry into my values and my heart that didn't just allow me to create the right legal documents for the care of my children, but turned me into a far better parent to them today. Focusing on the legacy you want to leave after you are gone, can and will make you a better parent today too.

It's so easy to get caught up in the day-to-day of parenting and work and relationships, that we lose sight of the gifts we really want to give our children. When we stop to consider the legacy we are leaving them, the lessons we want to pass on, the values, the insights, the stories and the experience – all so much greater than the money – we are able to incorporate that into our daily parenting. It changes us as parents.

When I first began to think seriously about what would happen to my children if something happened to me, I began by considering who I would want to raise them if I could not. But I quickly realized that merely focusing on who I wanted to raise my children alone would never be enough, because it really came down to how I wanted them raised.

And while I had given that a whole lot of thought from the

perspective of issues as they presented themselves, such as whether I would breastfeed or formula feed, how they would get to sleep at night and where they would sleep, and where they would go to preschool. …I really had not considered beyond the present moment.

How do you want your children raised at the ages of 6, 10, 13, and beyond? What would you want them to know if you weren't there to tell them or model for them? It's so easy to lose sight of what we really want to pass on to them. So much of what we pass on to our children is passed on unintentionally. They watch us. They see how we are in the world and they model it.

And what this means is we pass on patterns and conditioned ways of being that are not the real legacy we want to pass on to our children.

There is another way.

Instead, we can be intentional about the legacy we leave behind. By thinking now about what we want our children to experience, learn and grow from, we can take an ordinary experience of legal planning and turn it into something much greater. We can become intentional parents. Intentional parenting means you consciously focus on what you want to pass on to your children.

So, what do you want to pass on to your children?

Some of the things I realized I want my children to know are:

Number 1: they are enough. Whoever is raising them must start with that premise.

No matter what they do in the world, no matter what they want to do with their life, they are enough.

I want my children to know they do not have to take the traditional path. Anything they want to be or do with their life is fine with me, as long as they are passionate about it.

The greatest legacy I can leave my children is internal peace, a knowledge that no matter what/how they are taken care of, they don't have to fight for what's rightfully theirs, they already have it. There is nothing they want that they don't already have, not on the material or physical plane, but spiritually and emotionally. I want them to know that all their needs will be met from within.

As I thought through this legacy I wanted to leave them, I realized I had to begin parenting my children differently today. This isn't something that could wait until I died. And I also concluded that it ruled out the possibility of most people I knew raising them. These values and beliefs were simply not shared by most of the people in my family.

I would instead have to very carefully document who I wanted to raise my children, how I wanted them to be raised and why I chose the people I did, to ensure there would be no risk of fighting over my choice – in the event something did happen to me.

So here's what I did and you should do too …

First, I chose the people I would want to raise my children over the long term. I named my sister first, because I knew she would be most likely to be able to adopt these values and integrate them into her life if she became a parent to my children.

Then, I named two back-ups, in case she couldn't do it. Friends, not family. Friends I knew shared my core values. Next, I wrote very specific instructions to my potential guardians about how I would want them to raise my children, if it ever came to that.

After that, I created a document specifically excluding certain family members, who I knew would never be able to move out of their conditioned ways of thought that would trap my children in a life of convention and 'shoulds', if they were to be raised by them.

I created this document to ensure that all my family members who were not chosen would know why they were not chosen, and there would be no risk one of them would challenge the people I had named as guardians because they disapproved of my choice, which would create a nightmare for my children and the people I'd chosen to name as guardians.

Then, I began to develop a conscious relationship between my children and the people I had named as guardians. Some of the people I named were not people my children would have naturally spent a significant amount of time with, due to their life circumstances and distance from our family. Now with this foresight and planning, I was able to intentionally cultivate a relationship between these people and my children.

In at least one situation, I was led to change my guardian-nomination decision, when I realized that the people I had chosen were not quite as lined up with me as I thought they were. Who will raise your children is a decision to be revisited on a regular basis. As your children get older, their needs change and it's a constant process of re-evaluating who are the right people to raise them.

Once I had decided who I would want to raise my children for the long-term, I began to think about what would happen in the immediate term if something happened to me.

The people I had chosen as guardians all lived hundreds or thousands of miles away. So what would happen in the immediate term? My children were often home with a young babysitter who wouldn't know what to do or who to call if I didn't make it home.

As I thought that through, I faced the reality that my children could be taken into the care of strangers, at least until the authorities could figure out who I had named as guardians and how to reach them, unless I made alternative arrangements.

As a result, I decided I'd name guardians for the immediate-term. I chose people who live close by, who would be able to be at my house within 20 minutes if called upon. People my children knew and trusted. People I knew would be able to comfort my children until the people I named as permanent guardians arrived.

I then gave those people a legal document naming them as short-term, temporary guardians and told them to keep those documents somewhere accessible in case they were called upon. I created an ID card to carry in my wallet that listed the names and phone numbers of those local people and indicated on the card that I am a mom and I have minor children at home. I did this so that if I was in an accident, the authorities would know exactly who to contact if I could not communicate.

I then gave specific instructions to every person who cared for my children, including their babysitters, neighbors and school administrators to ensure there would be no risk that my children would be taken into the arms of strangers.

And last, but far from least, I recorded an audio CD for them – talking about all those things I wanted them to know if I wasn't there to tell them – I shared my values, my insights, my stories and the experiences I wanted to pass on. I physically created the legacy I wanted to leave them, so there would be no chance they wouldn't know what was most important to me.

By this time, I was an estate planning lawyer advising clients and after doing all of this for my children, I began incorporating this level of legacy planning into the estate plans I created for my clients. It's called a 'Kids Protection Plan' and you can create one for your children now. There's nothing stopping you from leaving a legacy to your children that is far greater than any amount of money you can leave behind.

If you have financial resources available to you, work with a lawyer specifically trained in working with families with young children, who can guide you to create your own Kids Protection Plan. You can find a lawyer like that at http://www.PersonalFamilyLawyer.com.

If you do not have financial resources, get started with naming legal guardians for your kids at http://www.KidsProtectionPlan.com.

It's free, it's easy and there's no excuses.

ABOUT ALEXIS

Alexis Martin Neely, Esq. is known as "The Truth-Telling Lawyer" because she tells it like it is, when it comes to what you really need to make sure your family and business are ready and able to grow in today's new economy.

Alexis is recognized as one of the nation's leading experts on legal planning for the needs of families and business owners. Her book **WEAR CLEAN Underwear** A Fast, Fun, Friendly – and Essential – Guide to Legal Planning for Busy Parents – is the national bestseller on the topic.

Alexis has appeared on television and radio networks throughout the country, including the Today Show, Good Morning America, CNBC's On the Money, CNN's O'Reilly Factor, and many more.

Alexis Neely, Esq. is a member of the California Bar. She holds a JD from Georgetown University, where she graduated first in her law school class.

In her spare time, Alexis spends her time with her children, Kaia and Noah.

To connect with Alexis:
Call: (866) 999-3974 OR contact her at:
Alexis@FamilyWealthMatters.com
Twitter.com/AlexisNeely
Facebook.com/PlayBigWithAlexis

CHAPTER 2

PERSPECTIVE

BY MARTHA J. HARTNEY, ESQ.

It's only when we truly know and understand that we have a limited time on earth – and that we have no way of knowing when our time is up – that we will begin to live each day to the fullest, as if it was the only one we had.

~ Elisabeth Kubler-Ross

I haven't been particularly struck by tragedy in life. What I've seen of life is simply the way it is—a cycle of birth, life, death, and rebirth; physically, metaphorically. Bearing witness to birth and death on many occasions has familiarized me with the path to and from the gateways of life. Of course, others have seen more of what I've seen—professional midwives, *doulas*, hospice care workers, doctors. Still, I've chosen the work I'm in because attending the entrances and exits in this life is a constant reminder to me to live fully and to help others do the same.

Here are two stories, out of many, about why I've chosen the work I do now.

****

Since my parents were much older than other parents and my father a pilot, I had a niggling fear that he might die early, earlier than other parents. My mom was 43 when I was born, my dad 46. For as long as I'd known, he had a heart condition, an electrical problem he refused to discuss. My parents didn't tell me for several years that my father had a pacemaker put in his chest, thinking that I would be better off not knowing. Of course, when I did find out, I felt left out of an important family event. I wouldn't let fear of death keep me from being present and accounted for in its company. That determination was tested pretty quickly.

In my first summer after college, I dated a young man I'd known for several years—Geoff. We'd met in a youth group as he struggled to heal from his sister's death in childbirth—wounds that our friendship comforted.

A few weeks into that summer, he asked me to the Fireman's Ball—he was a volunteer fireman like his dad, but a rookie of course. That night, he was puffed-up proud to show off his date at the local hotel ballroom. I'd never seen him smile quite so broadly. He was the kind of guy that guys like; immensely funny, self-effacing, loyal, but who's a little shy "with the ladies."

As it turned out, I'd been the first girl he dated for a couple years. And he'd been hoping for that chance for a while, patiently waiting for the right moment to ask me. After the ball, our first date, we continued to see each other, picnicked, went for walks, drove down to the Jersey shore. He was gentle, thoughtful, and not pushy when it came to physical affection as most guys are at that age. He was in love, and apparently had been for sometime. One afternoon, he'd asked me to go shopping with him to get his mother a birthday present. But I got called into work at the local ice cream shop so he went by himself.

Later that evening, a friend of ours came in to the restaurant where I worked, dragging me out into the parking lot, chocolate syrup smudges on my white apron.

"Martha," she said holding onto my shoulders, "Geoff's dead. He died today. In a car crash. Head-on collision with a truck." She tried to hold me up as my knees began to buckle.

The blood drained from my face. My stomach caved in and I fell over onto the blacktop. Gone.

****

When I graduated law school, I spent two months figuring out how to use the education I'd been given to serve kids and families. I asked my friends to tell me what they wanted to know about being a parent from a lawyer's perspective. I got quite a few responses, but only one took my breath away. It was from my cousin in the South – a story I was familiar with, but had not followed the details of into the present. Here is her story, abbreviated as it is…

My cousin wrote she wished she knew 16 years ago what she now knows. That is, once parents have kids, they should do everything they can to plan for the worst, plan for what happens when something happens to the parents.

When she was a new mom with a baby boy, her 18 year-old brother (my other cousin) and her husband had gone out to clean up an airplane that they were selling. They gave it one last wash and took it up to dry it off.

They never came back.

Eventually, the tears faded, the sorrow became less gripping—having lost both her brother and her husband in a flash. But in the midst of her suffering, she was hauled into probate court to deal with the assets he had left behind. And since then, she's been embroiled in probate even to this day. After 16 years, a financial guardian, bond payments, and court appearances, her once-infant son will soon be coming into his inheritance. All of it at once, at age 18.

He has shut her out. He doesn't want to talk to her. He moved in with another family member about an hour away. He knows he's getting his money and he will not listen to reason or good sense—it's not that he's a bad person—he's just young! He wants what he wants and he wants it now. There is no incentive for him to accept his mother's guidance because he will have his own source of funds—at least in the short term. And he will spend it. Hopefully, he will spend it wisely but even the wisest of children at that age can succumb to the pressures of a society that values 'stuff' more than people.

When my cousin and her husband had their son, they didn't plan for what would happen if one or both of them were taken away. Why would they have? They were young and vibrant and at the beginning of their life together.

And they're not alone. Most parents don't plan for the worst—69% don't. We just don't think it will happen to us. Who wants to think of themselves as mortal, fragile?

Years later, my cousin is still paying a far bigger price in heartache, hassle, worry and yes, money, than if she and her husband had found a way to afford a good estate plan that could grow and change with them as their family grew.

That was her message to me. Help people to do their estate planning right away, the right way, and keep it that way.

****

At last count, our family, where sons and daughters frequently choose careers in the sky, has lost three to airplane crashes; two young men, and one young woman. My brother also barely survived a B-52 crash. That's *four* in one family. What are the odds? Very slim yet there it is. Four.

Both my parents have passed away. They lived long and fruitful lives. My fear of losing them early never materialized. They didn't have to bear the suffering of surviving a child like my aunts and uncles did. I pray every day that I don't have to. And I pray every day that if something happens to me, my boys will be okay.

Fortunately, as an estate planning attorney, the very first plan I finished was my own. Now I have resources in place, owned in the right way, and I've written out exactly how I want my children to be raised and by whom. I've also provided the assets for my children's guardian to get them to college and hopefully, through college.

My estate will have to go to probate, but only for a small part of what I leave behind and for a short period of time. My family will not have to pay bond fees or unpredictable probate costs. They won't have to wait to use my assets. And they'll know exactly how to use those assets because I've left detailed instructions for my guardians and trustees.

Most of my assets are owned by my trust and will pass to my successor trustee immediately if something happens to me. There is no need to get court approval to pay my children's bills, no court-appointed financial guardian who doesn't know my children or me, no inheritance at 18.

Being a head of a second family, I've also made sure *my* estate provides for *my* kids. Ordinarily, at marriage, the spouse gets the bulk of their spouse's estate if no plan is in place.

That arrangement would leave my kids out in the cold and redirect my estate to my second husband and his children, and *vice versa*. Neither of us wants that.

Blended families, non-traditional families, same-sex families all need special planning to make sure that the ordinary rules of succession don't interfere with their need to provide for their own children first and foremost, then their second families.

Reflecting on my fear of my parents dying early, it wasn't so much about losing my parents. What worried me most was what would happen to us if something happened to my father. The possibility of him falling out of the sky was always present.

It's probably a very good thing that my parents survived my childhood because they didn't create a cohesive, thought-out plan for what would happen to their 10 children if something happened to them. Very likely, we'd have been tossed around in the juvenile system, without resources, raised by someone a judge picked out, not by someone my parents loved and trusted. The opportunity to go to college would have evaporated, as may have the opportunities I've had later in life that built on my early life – to give birth and raise two beautiful sons, to travel, to learn new things, to go to law school.

That's why I've chosen this work, to help moms and dads understand what their children would experience if they don't plan, and to help them plan so they and their children never have to fear as I did.

Most of us will never need to put an estate plan into action. If all goes according to schedule, we will live well beyond our children's youth, see them date, start a life, and have their own families. …Mission accomplished.

It sounds trite to say "I do estate planning for families with children," because it's so much more than that. It's helping parents preserve their treasures, spiritual and material, so that their kids can get the most out of their childhood regardless of the hand they draw. It's recognizing the importance of each child's gift to the world and helping parents make sure that he or she has every opportunity to bring it to fulfillment. It's minding the gates of life.

So instead of saying I do estate planning for families with children, it would be more helpful to say I help parents face death, so that they can live life fully now and be better parents for it.

ABOUT MARTHA

Hartney Family & Estate Law is an estate planning practice serving all kinds of Colorado families. A later-in-life attorney, Martha Hartney opened the practice in 2010 to serve the people she loves because she is committed to helping moms and dads bring their greatest gifts into parenting fearlessly and with joy and making sure children are completely cared for if something happens to their parents.

Martha graduated from the University of Denver while being a full time mother of two sons. She focused her studies on family, juvenile, and estate law and served in the Boulder County District Attorney's Office; Larimer County Domestic Courts; and the Rocky Mountain Children's Law Center. Martha has served as a pro bono guardian ad litem representing abused and delinquent children. After law school, she was certified as a Child & Family Investigator through the Colorado Bar Association. She has also supported new mothers as a La Leche League Leader and been an advocate of attachment parenting and natural parenting.

CHAPTER 3

LESSONS LEARNED THE HARD WAY

BY RICHARD S. CARLYON, ESQ.

Do you have an estate plan? No? How about a "living will" or lifetime trust? Not that either? Well, how about a trust for your children or grandchildren? Nope? Just a simple will? Uh, not that either?

You would be simply amazed how many people living in the United States today would answer the series of questions above in just the same way – "no" to all of them. How can that be, you ask? Doesn't everyone have at least a will? No-where close. Experts estimate that of the competent (a/k/a not mentally ill) adults in this country, age thirty-five and older, who have any worldly possessions to pass on to some-one else upon their own death, fewer than twenty percent have any kind of estate plan, trust, will or other plan of their own making for passing their property on to others. And the number is only a hair better for those in their forties. Even the older crowd, those fifty years old and up don't do much better, with less than half of them having some type of legal, organized plan for the distribution of their assets upon their own death. "No!" you cry in disbelief. "That can't be true!" you exclaim. "What about mom and dad?" you wonder, "and rich Uncle Louie?" – surely he's made plans to leave me something. Nope. Don't count on it.

Those experts who tally this type of data typically say that if you haven't done it by age forty, you probably won't ever prepare any type of estate plan, including a simple will. Now there is some hope, it's typically known by the general category of "Life Insurance." "Of course!" you cry with glee, "I knew that my grandparents wouldn't forget me – they're both loaded up with AARP life insurance!"

There are at least three major problems with life insurance from a purely estate planning perspective. (1): Many plans are straight term life that expire at a certain age. (2): The owner of a policy of life insurance with cash value may, in most cases, borrow against that cash value, leaving nothing payable at their death, and (3): Many, many people make the mistake of naming "my estate" as the primary beneficiary under the life insurance that they buy. What's wrong with that, you ask? Two things. Even as part of a well thought out estate plan, if the life insurance is payable to the decedent's (a fancy word for dead person) estate, it may increase the total value of the estate to the point that it may become taxable under state and/or federal inheritance tax statutes. This in turn may take a big bite out of the estate remaining for distribution to the devisees (another fancy term – this time for those named to inherit under the will, trust, or similar dispositive [oops, another one slipped in here somehow] document).

The third major problem with insurance benefits payable "to

my estate," is that unless you have some type of estate plan (including, at a minimum, a simple will) in place, then there is nowhere for this insurance money to go — except into a large hole we sometimes call "descent and distribution," which means that the decedent's estate is distributed by a formula concocted by your state legislature — a statute — and not necessarily the way in which the decedent would have directed, if they had bothered to do so. (But there are many good ways the various forms of life insurance may be used as part of your over-all estate plan.)

How do we know all this? Well, first I must make clear that the distribution of decedent's estates, whether by estate plan or by descent and distribution, is purely a matter of state law. What happens in California doesn't necessarily happen in Texas, and New York is going to be different, and so are most of the states in one way or another. But there are some general facts common to almost every state; such as the number of people with no planning of any kind in place to handle the inevitable. And how do we know about that, you say? Here's where the second caveat (a disclaimer, you know, 'C-Y-A') is proper. All of these facts and figures quoted to you above are based on historical data. The experts don't really know the percentage of *living* forty year-olds that don't have a will. They must rely upon the recorded history of those who have gone before us ("historical data").

Oh, so now you think that surely your parents' generation is much more enlightened and savvy about these things and have made proper and ample arrangements for your care in the manner in which you have become accustomed (not always a good thing). Unfortunately, the experts' review of this data over long periods of time shows little improvement in the propensity for otherwise rational human beings to put an estate plan in place to answer the burning questions such as "who gets Aunt Sophie's antique chair?" when they die. We can send a man to the moon, but we can't make people create a will.

Psychologists, cultural anthropologists, and other experts who have studied this tendency of modern man to avoid the rational act of setting up some type of estate plan – be it grandiose or a very simple two page will, have not reached a final answer to this question. But, they have several good hypotheses for man's apparent dislike for the estate planning process. The most common answer given by the experts is that the processes of planning how one's estate will be handled upon their death forces one to face his or her own mortality, which many people apparently don't like to think about. Some people go as far as to say its bad luck to plan for the distribution of a person's estate. Some even say that if you plan for it, it will happen soon thereafter.

There is no conclusive scientific evidence of any connection between estate planning and the actual occurrence of death, but that doesn't seem to stop some people from using that excuse for why they don't execute a plan. Others fear the cost of an estate plan. An estate plan can be as expensive or as affordable as you like and even the least expensive and simple estate plan is better than having a state statute and a probate court decide where your assets go upon your death. Some people say that they laugh out loud when they think about their greedy heirs fighting over their estates once they pass, and feel that the greedy heirs have what's coming to them for being so unpleasant. I doubt that a definitive answer will ever be agreed upon by the experts, but the point is that no matter how distasteful the planning process is to a person, they owe it to their heirs, and many would say that they owe it to *society*, whether or not they have any heirs, to at least prepare a simple will disposing of their entire estate upon their death.

Those who argue that society should demand that a person plan their estate cite to the clogging of our court systems with otherwise unnecessary court hearings and litigation – had there been a proper will or estate plan in place prior to the decedent's death and to the unclaimed money that ends up in the state's coffers by escheat ("by operation of law") since there were no heirs identified to distribute the money too. If you don't want to give it to your greedy heirs then at least leave it to a charity, they argue.

Now that you've had some time to digest all of this, the little lawyer in your head (yes, we all have one – they're everywhere) pipes up and says "so what?" What is so terrible about those who die without leaving behind a will or other estate-planning device? In most states and in most cases the heirs of those who die intestate (sorry, "without a will") must go to court, usually a probate court or family court of some type, and have the legitimacy of the decedent's heirs determined by a judge, or sometimes by a jury! The court may even order certain assets sold and others given to one particular heir instead of another, and so on. This can get quite contentious, especially if you really wanted Aunt Sophie's antique chair, and your rotten brother got it instead. There have been many family feuds over a dead relative's possessions. It often leads to litigation over who gets what, or who is really related to whom. It has been known to lead to bloodshed and even to murder. Sounds like a plot from an Agatha Christie novel, doesn't it? The saying that "truth is stranger than fiction" had to come from somewhere, didn't it? Well, I think it came out of probate court.

Let me give you a real life example:

Amos Able (not his real name) married his high school sweetheart, Alice (not her real name, either) when he got back from World War Two (now that part is real). Like many returning veterans of WWII, Amos and Alice got right down to the business of creating a family – the old fashioned way. Soon they had three lovely children, ages 3, 5, and 7; but soon Amos had a wandering eye.

After a couple of "trial" adulterous relationships, Amos finally found one that stuck, and moved out of his and Alice's happy home into the *so* much happier house owned by Betty Bishop (yeah, not her real name either), a very attractive divorced young woman with no children. Although Betty had divorced her first husband and taken back her maiden name, Amos was not so efficient or thoughtful; but he was consistent. Betty soon gave Amos three more children: Amos, Jr., Ralph (named after a Navy buddy), and Susie Lee, who everyone just called "Sissy." (You guessed it – not their real names either.)

The strange thing is that Betty's house was only four blocks away from where Alice still lived with her three children (all compliments of Amos Sr.'s post-war amour), and they all used to see each other on the street, at school, at the store, and so on – but neither Alice nor Amos, Sr. ever sued for divorce.

We can't ask Amos, Sr., since he is the decedent in this story, but according to his first wife, Alice, they never got divorced because of the religious teachings of a certain church they were married in and both attended until Amos, Sr. took his leave. I'm not going to touch that subject folks, but that's the way it was – "sure as shootin'!"

Wait a minute; I said "according to his first wife, Alice,"

above, didn't I. Well that's a mistake (in more ways than one!) as Alice and Amos, Sr. were never divorced, and Amos, Sr. and Betty were never formally married, and didn't fit the definition of a "common-law marriage" in the state where they all lived since Amos, Sr. and Alice were legally married up until the day Amos died.

Here's where things start to get sticky. Amos, Sr. had two "families" when he died, but only one legal wife. Amos, Sr. only lived with Alice for nine years and was a carpet salesman during that whole time. However, he lived with Betty almost forty years, and became a prosperous real estate investor during their time together (another absolutely true set of facts).

One day, after all six of his children were legal "grown-ups," and just shy of the fortieth anniversary of the day he moved in with Betty, Amos, Sr. fell dead of a massive heart attack while walking home from work. Even though his two "families" lived 'within spittin' distance' of each other all of these years, they had pretty much stayed away from each other. The first three children claimed Alice as their mother and only parent and Amos, Jr., Ralph, and Sissy claimed Amos, Sr. as their father and only parent. All of that was about to change.

Even though Amos Sr.'s earthly remains hadn't yet cooled off sufficiently at the coroner's office for the autopsy to begin, things were starting to heat up fast and furious between the two "families" he had left behind. His first three children had decided that their poor old dad, who they had only seen occasionally during his almost forty years with Betty, wasn't such a bad guy after all – especially since he was now dead and (by their standards) filthy rich. Family number two was devastated that their "Papa," as they called him, had left them before giving each of them a $100,000.00 certificate of deposit at the local savings and loan association, as he had promised to do on a regular basis. Oh poor Papa was gone, what were they to do, and Mama, where is Papa's will? Good question.

About that same time, Amos, Sr.'s first three children, led by the oldest, a son, Butch, were asking their mother the same question. Everyone managed to get through the funeral without a fight, but the accusations and threats began to fly soon after the grave of Amos, Sr., was closed. The problem both women faced was the same – neither Alice nor Betty knew where Amos' will was located. He had told both women that they would "be taken care of for the rest of their lives" in his will. But none of the women dared ask the hot-headed Amos where the will was actually located, and no one had ever seen the will, although several of the children would swear differently in court later.

Amos, Jr. came to see me just after a year had passed since his father's death. He had fired his first attorney and was looking for someone else to represent his mother, his brother, Sissy, and himself in the suit they had filed through the first attorney almost nine months ago in the probate proceeding initiated by Alice and her children, to have the court determine heirship and distribute the assets, as no will of Amos, Sr. was ever located. The original attorney had made some far-reaching arguments that were, in some cases, hard to substantiate under the law of the state in question and the facts of this particular case. But it was enough to keep the probate court from automatically ruling in favor of Alice and her children, and that was enough in the beginning. But later, Amos Jr. and the rest of his family wanted more than a delaying tactic – they actually wanted *all* of their father's earthly possessions. I told him up front that getting it all for the "second family" was unlikely. I told him a lot of things up front that he seemed to forget eighteen months later.

One of the valuable lessons that came out of the case known as *In Re: the estate of Amos Able, Sr., Deceased,* was that when a potential client has already had one or more lawyers there is a good chance you won't be the last lawyer to handle the case. That's not exactly what happened here though. I was a young lawyer, eager and hungry, so I took the case, even though I had some misgivings from the start.

After about a year of pre-trial written discovery, a couple of depositions, and three or four hearings before the probate court, we were not much closer to getting any inheritance for Betty and her children than when we started. One of the problems was that Sissy, yes sweet little sister Sissy, was in and out of jail the whole time I handled this case, making obtaining her testimony and assistance difficult, at best.

When we reached the one-year mark of my tenure as one of the attorney's in this case, and with things not looking much better than they had in the beginning, I told Amos, Jr. that we should try and cut a deal with our opponents. He was very angry at first. He told me I was a lousy lawyer and that I just wanted to take the easy way out. Rant, rant, rant, etc. Then he thought it over, looked at how much his family had spent on the case, and came back to me with an "OK."

I had reasoned with him that the law and the facts just weren't on his side in this case. That hasn't kept good lawyers from winning cases before, but it sure makes it more difficult. Since Amos, Sr. and Alice had never been legally divorced during his lifetime, she was his legal spouse at the time of his death under the state statute for descent and distribution, which, at that time stated that the surviving spouse, where there was no will, would receive her one half of the couple's community property, and one half of all of her deceased spouse's property, be it community or separate property, and that the remaining one half of the decedent's property would be divided equally between the children born from the marriage between the decedent and his spouse at the time of death. So this meant everything went to Alice and her children, even though Amos, Sr. had lived almost four times longer with Betty and her children.

Amos, Jr.'s first attorney had argued that the probate court should act "in equity" and consider the forty years Amos, Sr. had spent with Betty. This living together for an extended period of time and holding each other out to the public as man and wife satisfied all but one of the state statute's major requirements for a common law marriage, and that was that neither the putative husband nor wife could still be legally married to another person during the time they claimed to be married by common law. If Amos, Sr. and Alice had gotten a legal divorce before his death, this problem might have been avoided. The sure bet was for him (and his "second family") to have executed a proper and legal **Last Will and Testament** in which he could have divided his one half of his community property (if any) and all of his separate property between whomever he wanted.

But he didn't and both of his "families" suffered because of it. Once Amos, Jr. agreed to try and settle, it took another six months to negotiate a truce. By that time, both sides had learned that Amos, Sr. was not as wealthy as everyone thought. He had a gambling and a drinking problem and had borrowed heavily against his real estate empire to pay his debts. By the time both sides of this dispute had paid their lawyers, there was little left for anyone to inherit.

The moral of this story is simple. A proper will, which would have cost Amos, Sr. about $250.00 at the time, would have solved all of this immediately upon his death. Sure, anybody can sue anybody else, just about anytime for anything – but it would have been very difficult for anyone to win under these circumstances against a properly appointed Independent Executor (or Executrix) who was acting in accordance with the law under Amos, Sr.'s properly drawn and executed *Last Will and Testament*.

So there you have it. Whether you like it or not, your heirs will thank you if you draw up a proper estate plan that could be as simple as a two page will. Even if you don't like your potential heirs, you can show your dislike for them even more by setting up an estate plan that gives everything to someone else or to a charity or public cause. Don't tie up the probate courts with needless will contests and litigation – do the responsible thing and at least have a simple will drawn up. I haven't even touched on the other many positive aspects of a proper estate plan; such as tax savings, protecting your estate from you and your heir's creditors, or from a divorce in your lifetime, or among one or more of your heirs.

ABOUT RICHARD

Richard Scott Carlyon, Esq, has been practicing law for 20 years in general business, real estate, litigation, and estate planning. He advises entrepreneurs and small to mid-sized businesses, particularly family-owned businesses, to help them either structure their business properly from the start or if they're already up and running, get them on the right track. This means setting up the proper type of entity for the business, providing succession and asset protection planning. He also works to make sure they have good banking, investment, insurance and accounting support, and then acts as their "part-time" in-house counsel.

Scott has found that many people starting out in business (as well as many small to mid-sized business owners) are poorly advised on the value of lawyers and the cost of consulting with one. This often winds up as the saying goes, "pay me now or pay me later." He states that its less expensive, and certainly less stressful, to set things up right from the start, and to have ready access to an attorney to review business strategies, contracts, etc. in advance, than it is to wait until the business has a problem, or is sued, to go looking for an attorney.

Before he practiced law, he ran a holding company that owned a bank, a mortgage lender, and a real estate brokerage company. At that company, he had 120 employees and an executive staff of 12. He had at least six lawyers on retainer at all times, so he knows what its like to be sitting in the client's chair in an attorney's office and having a deposition taken, etc.

Scott wants you to know that its less expensive, easier, and less stressful to consult with a lawyer before you jump into a business deal than it is to go to one when the deal has fallen apart.

CHAPTER 4

HOW TO LEAVE A LEGACY THAT LASTS...

BY KRISTINA R. HAYMES, ESQ.

This we know to be true – one day we will all die and our time on this earth will end. We know this truth but we don't think about it regularly. We don't think about it regularly not because we do not care about what will happen to our children, grandchildren, family, spouse, or loved ones after we die, but we don't think about it because we are too busy with the business of life! Life is busy. As an estate planning lawyer, business owner, wife, and mother of three boys, I know this to be true.

Yet, here is something I also know to be true – if you live your life knowing, conscious that today could be your last, that no one is promised tomorrow, how you live your life today will change. You will live differently and you may even choose **to be different**. If you knew that you were dying tomorrow, would you love more? Would you focus on what really matters? The lens of your life would become much more focused on **life priorities** such as where you will go when you die, and how you should really live. Did you do what you were put on this earth to do (did your life matter)? …did you love? …and did you choose eternity?

My dad passed away suddenly while on a fishing trip in Alaska. For him, it was probably a peaceful and easy way to go. For me, it was shocking, profoundly upsetting and heart breaking. My father had prepared a trust many years before; yet, it was never updated by his attorney before he died. He attempted to amend it himself a few short weeks before he died. His trust was not fully funded – some assets were owned outside of trust. Notwithstanding the fact that in some ways his financial affairs and his estate plan were a bit of a mess, those things could be fixed with some time and money.

Of far greater concern was the loss of my dad's real essence – which had little to do with his trust, or his real estate, his business, or his other assets – his real essence was wrapped up in his intangible wealth. You see, there was so much more to my dad and his legacy than his estate. The true value of my dad's life was his spiritual, emotional, psychological, and familial legacy. My dad wanted to leave a legacy and he did! He knew he would not live forever. But I wish that instead of just being imprinted upon my heart and my memory, that my dad had left a more concrete recording. Not just for me but for my children! My youngest child was two-and-a-half years old when my dad died. So really, while he sees pictures of himself with Grandpa, he doesn't really remember him. To him, his Grandpa's voice is silent.

How I would love for my three boys to be able to learn from the incredible wisdom and life lessons that Grandpa could share. My dad was a spiritual leader in our family. He was a man of great faith and great generosity. He coached me in soccer for years, earned a Ph.D. in psychology and was a teacher of the power of visualization and positive thinking. How I long to have my boys learn from a male role model like that.

Someone at one point, when my dad had been diagnosed with cancer, had said to me, "you should video tape him." Unfortunately, I never did. I moved to New Jersey and he was home in Encinitas, California. He was cured of the cancer, but his heart would one day fail.

I desire to live a life of no regrets; yet, I feel the void. I am sad that my boys cannot hear Grandpa's voice and listen to him share his wealth of wisdom, his life stories, and a special message for them.

Your legacy while you are living is about the investment that you make during your life into people and into projects. Your legacy is who you were, what you did and how you loved. Once you are gone, your legacy is that which lives on. Those families with wealth may choose to create charitable foundations to create a legacy. This is a great way to help enrich the lives of others and do well by doing good. But don't think you need to have millions of dollars to create a legacy that lasts. Everyone has something of value to share. You are unique, and you have wisdom from your years of living, life lessons, stories and experiences. You have a message for your descendants that could enrich their lives immeasurably.

What would it mean to my son to hear from his Grandpa that his grandfather prayed for him and the life he would have – while he was in his mother's womb? Would it give him hope and purpose, and help him to understand his life has meaning? What would it mean to my son to hear from his grandfather that " the word 'can't' is not in my vocabulary" and to have one of Grandpa's lessons on believing in yourself and the power of your words? What would it mean to my sons to hear from another male in their bloodline about success, and how to succeed in life and business? What would it mean to my son to hear his Grandpa's voice on faith and what really matters? I have no doubt that much was lost because I did not record a video or other message from my dad to my children. Yet, I can attempt to recreate what I can with the messages I remember.

Additionally now, I am passionate about helping others create their legacies that last. I don't want anyone to miss out on the opportunity to pass on their legacy. I don't want my loss to be yours. All of our estate planning clients can record a legacy video conversation where they are invited to share a special message for their children or grandchildren. My clients on our membership program can record a new video each year and choose from a variety of different topics. This exercise will someday enrich the lives of others. Right now, this exercise will also help you to focus on what really matters to you. It provides a gentle reminder to yourself of your mortality and how you choose to live.

Someday your loved ones will treasure these recordings just as much, if not more than any material assets you leave behind. Money comes and goes, but wisdom and true wealth lasts forever. It is a small thing, yet, someday for someone, it could mean the world.

Create Legacies that Last Today.

ABOUT KRISTINA

Kristina R. Haymes, Esq. has been a lawyer for over a decade. She graduated from one of the country's top-ten law schools, the University of California, Berkeley (Boalt Hall) School of Law (now known as **Berkeley Law**). Kristina began her legal career at premier, international firms in San Francisco. She then practiced in New Jersey when her husband, Dr. Cesar Haymes, took their family to the East Coast for his medical residency. While in New Jersey, Kristina also became a **mediator** participating in training at Pepperdine's Straus Institute and at Harvard, and she worked resolving litigation, family business, real estate, and trust and estate disputes outside of court.

Kristina loves being back in San Diego where she grew up, and now combines her passion for law and mediation with her **trust and estate practice in her firm, Haymes Law Group.** Kristina's mission is to empower and equip families to protect their wealth, provide for and protect their minor children were something to happen, and to create legacies that last by passing on more than material wealth to future generations.

Kristina's goal is to be your family's trusted advisor and to assist you in making the best legal, financial, and business decisions throughout your life and to be there to guide your loved ones when you cannot be.

Kristina lives in San Diego with her husband and three boys and they enjoy playing soccer, tennis, swimming, and going to the beach. Kristina has volunteered as an advisory board member for the Boys & Girls Club Montessori School, raised funds for her local church, and coaches youth soccer.

Education:

UC Berkeley Boalt Hall School of Law (Berkeley Law), JD 1999
University of New Mexico, Albuquerque, MA 1996 *with distinction*
University of California Santa Barbara, BA 1993

Kristina R. Haymes, Esq. can be located at: www.HaymesLawGroup.com and you can sign up for her free reports and videos at: www.SanDiegoEstatePlan.net.

CHAPTER 5

IF ONLY THEY HAD KNOWN…

EVALUATING AN ESTATE FROM A PERSONAL PERSPECTIVE

BY KYRA FISCHBECK HOWELL, ESQ

John loved his farm. He loved the land, he loved the smell of the hay, he loved his orchard. People from all over came to his orchard for the sweet taste of peaches, apples and pears. They came for the sense of peace and simplicity that the country life offered them, if only for an hour or so. It's beauty and calming nature could not be disputed.

John's plan was to have his daughter, Francesca, take over the farm operations when he was no longer able. She loved the land as much as he did. She was able to direct the pickers with efficiency, manage the books, and she loved it enough to keep the farm in the family. John's wife had passed away from cancer five years before, and Francesca had grown up in a short time helping her father with many of the household duties.

John just assumed that when he passed, the farm would go to Francesca and had said as much through his will, which he had drawn up by the local attorney. They had decided that that he could leave the farm to Francesca, and leave his other financial investments, except for the farm savings account, to his son Jared. Jared was in business school and didn't have much interest in the farm. But he had a good head on his shoulders, and John felt confident that Jared would invest his inheritance wisely, maybe even starting his own business venture.

John liked the local attorney. He had been in the town for about twenty-five years, and most everyone did business with him. There had never been any real disputes with his legal services; he did just fine in his general practice. John just assumed that his estate plan was what it needed to be with the advice of an attorney. That's what they're supposed to do, right?

Two years passed after John had his will drawn up, and he got remarried to a woman he had known practically his whole life. She knew his children and they all got along pretty well. Francesca was now able to concentrate more on the business of the farm, which made her happy, and everything seemed to be going smoothly.

Then John was in an accident. A tragic accident with his tractor while mowing down the hayfield. He died almost instantly. Shock hit the family, and they were devastated by their loss. Francesca felt the heavy burden of his loss most of all, as her father, friend, and business mentor were now gone. The farm was hers now. His legacy and her responsibility. She loved it even more, for she suddenly saw her father's years of hard work everywhere she looked. Her work on the farm became a labor of love far beyond her love for the land. It was to honor everything he had put into this land and to ensure his legacy continued.

The week after John's funeral, his widow, Clara, was left empty and confused, wondering where her place was now that he was gone. She was not the mother to his children, and she had never gotten around to talking with him about a will. She knew he had one, but she didn't want to be nosy to see what it contained. What was in it for her? But now she had to know. Where was she supposed to go from here? She assumed she would inherit the house from her husband. But Francesca also lived there. Would they continue to have that arrangement now?

She decided to contact the attorney to see if he had John's will so they could start to get the proper affairs in order. So on a Thursday, Clara sat down with the attorney to hear the contents of John's will.

"Clara," the attorney said, "I have looked at John's will which was drawn up a few years ago and realized that I should actually be talking to Francesca about the will. She is named Executor of John's estate."

"Francesca?" Clara said. "Didn't John update the will when we got married?"

"No, he didn't," the attorney said.

"But you knew we got married, right?" Clara asked in disbelief.

"Sure, I knew. But it's up to the client to let me know when they want to make a change to their documents. I can't keep up with everyone's life changes. If I did that, I wouldn't have time to practice law!" The attorney said with a chuckle.

Clara felt hopeless and panicked. "But what does this mean for me?" Clara asked him.

"I'm afraid you're going to have to hire another attorney, Clara. Since I was John's lawyer, I will naturally be helping Francesca with his estate. Working with you would be a conflict of interest for me. I'll be happy to give you the names and numbers of a couple of other attorneys who might be able to help you." He said as he jotted some names and numbers down on a piece of paper.

"Uh, okay. Thanks." Clara mumbled, not sure what to think or do at that moment. Suddenly she felt more lost without John than ever. As she went to the door, the attorney said "Now don't forget to tell Francesca to come see me."

"Sure thing," Clara responded as she exited the door, knowing full well that she had no intention of doing so until she knew what her next step should be.

Back at the farm, Francesca was trying to figure out what to do with her father's things. She knew there must be a will somewhere that she had to file for legal purposes. She had looked through her father's desk, but had not found it there. She had, however, found his attorney's business card – Bert W. Atkins, Esquire. So she decided to give him a call to see what he knew and if he would help her sort through whatever she needed to do.

Bert Atkins answered the phone at his law office and heard Francesca Watson on the other end calling to inquire about her father's will.

"I'm glad Clara delivered the message to you to call me,"

said Mr. Atkins. "I wasn't sure how she was feeling about the information I had given her."

"What?" asked a confused Francesca. "Clara didn't tell me anything. I found your card in my father's desk," said Francesca.

"Oh, hmm" said Mr. Atkins. "Well then, you had better come on down and see me so I can help you get things straightened out. I was so sorry to hear about your father's accident."

"Thank you, Mr. Atkins. I'll come by tomorrow," said Francesca, now more anxious than ever to know what was going on.

"That'll be fine, right before lunch," confirmed Mr. Atkins.

As she hung up the phone, Francesca sank into her father's old chair and felt exhausted. Exhausted from emotion, from her work on the farm, and from the suddenly heavy burden on her heart about a possible problem with Clara. She and Clara had gotten along just fine, but now she wasn't so sure it would stay that way.

Why didn't Clara give her the message to call the lawyer? What was she hiding? Francesca was determined to find out and knew that no matter what, she could not let her father's farm suffer in the process.

The next day was Tuesday, and around 11 a.m. Francesca went down to Mr. Atkins' office to hear the contents of her father's will. She was incredibly nervous, and just kept telling herself not to get too carried away in her mind with what the results could be. She just simply had to get through this meeting to know what to do next.

Mr. Atkins guided Francesca into his small conference room – a table with four chairs around it and a potted plant that needed watering. He had a folder open in front of him that had her father's name on it. Just looking at it overwhelmed her with sadness again at his loss.

"Okay, Francesca," Mr. Atkins started. "I don't know if your father ever shared the contents of his will with you, but I'm going to now just so you know everything there is to know, okay?"

"Sure. He never did tell me about it. So I really have no idea," said Francesca quietly.

"No problem. It's pretty simple really. Your father left you the farm and everything that goes with it, including the farm's bank account. And he left all of his other investments and accounts to your brother, Jared. You are named executor of his estate, so it will be your responsibility to get things filed with the Court to probate his will. I'll help you, of course," the attorney said.

Francesca sat quietly for a moment, trying to process what this really meant for her life, for her brother, and finally for Clara. What about Clara? Bert Atkins hadn't mentioned anything about her. But she had already been to see him. She had to know.

"What about my father's wife, Clara?" she asked.

"Your father drew up his will before he married Clara. He never updated it. She is not mentioned in his will. She wanted to know when she came by what she could expect from his estate. But you are the executor, so I told her that I had to talk with you about the contents of his will. I suggested that she get another attorney since I would be helping you out. I don't want there to be a conflict of interest on my part," he said matter-of-factly.

"Of course not," Francesca answered. "So if she is not named in the will, she gets nothing?" she asked.

"She will have to go to court to request her share as his wife, and by statute they will give her something. But I would imagine that between the accounts you and Jared are inheriting, you'll be able to take care of that."

"Court?" Francesca asked in disbelief. "You mean I'll have to go to court against Clara over this? How long will that take?" Francesca asked.

"Well, probate takes quite a bit of time. Usually a year or so, especially with the judge having to get involved in the omitted spouse statutory question," Bert answered.

"A year! We have to go through this for another year?" Francesca asked in disbelief.

"At least," he replied. "That's if it all goes smoothly. But I've seen these things drag on for at least two years, and that's not uncommon."

Francesca couldn't believe what she was hearing. She knew that one to two years in court, tied up in probate, would be costly to the farm. Even with her brother's share helping out with the expenses. It would not only cost them financially, it would cost them emotionally and mentally with the drawn-out process depleting their time, energy, and ability to move forward in their lives as best they could after this tragedy.

"Thank you, Mr. Atkins. I need time to think about all of this. It's just hard to process all of it. Would you write up your recommendations for me and let me know what I need to do next? I'll be back in touch in a few days."

"Sure will, Francesca. I'm sorry to have to break it to you like this. But probate is never easy. Especially where a will has not been kept up-to-date," he answered.

"Isn't there any other way this could have been handled to avoid this situation?" she had to ask.

"Yes, some people put their assets in a trust, which is meant to avoid probate. But your father just wanted a simple will. That what he asked for," the lawyer answered.

As Francesca left the attorney's office, she couldn't help but wonder what her day would have been like if her father had put his assets into a trust instead of going through probate, and if he had kept his documents up-to-date every year to account for changes in his life. There must be an attorney out there who would have helped him do this, right?

If only they had known…

ABOUT KYRA

Kyra Fischbeck Howell, Esq.'s estate and business planning practice focuses on helping families enhance their lives today and securing their futures tomorrow. She excels in guiding her clients through the often confusing maze of financial and legal decisions to create plans that ensure the well-being of their families and the accomplishment of cherished family goals. Her legal services include family protection, wealth preservation, and values-based planning, as well as planning strategies for unmarried couples and divorced individuals. Whether you are married or single, have a traditional family or blended one, just starting out or looking back on a life well-lived, Kyra will help you craft a plan that achieves your goals for your loved ones today and for years to come.

Kyra graduated in the top one-third of her law school class from Fordham University School of Law in 1996, having attended at night, and served as Director of Business Affairs and in-house counsel to PrimeTime 24, an entertainment company in New York City, from 1996 to 1998. Kyra then moved to Virginia and was selected as assistant telecommunications counsel to the Ranking Member of the U.S. House of Representatives' Commerce Committee. She then served as Legislative Assistant in the United States Senate to Senator Frank Lautenberg, handling among other things, small business and taxation issues. After leaving Capitol Hill, Kyra was an associate at the law firm of Powell, Goldstein, Frazer & Murphy, where she represented companies in international trade and intellectual property legislative matters. Kyra is the founder of The Howell Law Firm , PLLC, which opened in 2005, and she now pursues her interests of working closely with individuals by engaging in planning for parents and grandparents focused on the healthy transition of family wealth. Kyra is a member of the Estates & Trusts Section of the American Bar Association as well as the Virginia Bar Association.

Kyra's previous work has been quoted in the Washington Post, and she has appeared in the media – including MSNBC, CBC-Toronto, and Radio Free Europe. Kyra has chosen to concentrate on Trusts and Estates and Business Planning, because she is passionate about helping families create happy and secure futures.

Most importantly, Kyra and her husband Steven are the proud parents of Mason, Lilliane, and Carson.

P.O. Box 228, Sperryville, Virginia 22740
www.thehowelllawfirm.com
P: 877-351-5732
F: 571-921-4304

CHAPTER 6

LEGACY OF LOVE – PART I

THE VALUE OF EMOTIONAL ASSETS

BY GEMINI ADAMS

When the idea for *Your Legacy of Love* first came to mind, a seed of doubt still rattled around in my head. I didn't inherit such a legacy from Mom, and at the time, didn't actually know anyone who had. Despite my conviction that this would help to reduce the mental and emotional suffering of grief, I wasn't sure if my own needs were the same as others who had experienced such a loss. I needed to know that this would really benefit the bereaved to ensure I wasn't proposing something that might actually do more harm than good. So in addition to my desk research, I started an independent survey asking the question:

What would you prefer if one of your parents died: to inherit their wealth or a letter saying how much they loved you?

I quizzed people from all walks of life and asked them to pass this question on to their family and friends. Kindly they agreed to help, and I soon received over two hundred and fifty replies. They came from Europe, America, Canada, Asia and Australia, with responses from business people, parents, children, professionals, servicemen and women, doctors, lawyers, homemakers, artists, musicians and engineers—the majority of whom had already lost someone close to them.

WHY MEANINGFUL WORDS WIN OVER MONEY

It was a relief to discover that I wasn't alone. Over ninety percent of these people expressed a wish to have some words preserved on paper. Of the tiny minority who didn't want a letter, one woman joked that if there was a chance she might inherit a château in the south of France, she would have to take it (there's always one!). Perhaps she never saw the film *Billy Elliot*—which illustrates the power of a simple message for surviving family members. *Billy Elliot* is the story of a young boy growing up in the north of England during the miners' strikes of the early '80s. He struggles to cope with the loss of his mother and to deal with his father's grief at having lost both his wife and his job. Unknown to Billy, his mother wrote him a letter before she died, leaving instructions for it to be presented to him on his eighteenth birthday. Concerned about him and his behavior, his Grandmother prematurely delivers the gift, hoping it will encourage his recovery. Billy is just eleven when he receives his mother's letter:

To My Son Billy,

I know that I must seem like a distant memory to you, which is probably a good thing. It will have been a long time and I will have missed seeing you grow, missed you crying, laughing and shouting and I will have missed telling you off. But please know that I was always there with you, through everything, and I always will be. I am proud to have known you, and I am proud that you were mine. Always be yourself, I love you forever.

Mom

These kind and encouraging words have a potent effect on young Billy. The support and appreciation he receives from his mother through this letter seems to give him the strength to fight the cultural and familial battles that prevented him from pursuing his passion for ballet, the only thing he loves. He shares the precious letter with his dance teacher, Mrs.Wilkinson, the one person who seems to believe in him. Moved by what she reads, Mrs.Wilkinson begins helping Billy to develop his talent for dancing, while encouraging him to do something he would never otherwise have dreamed of: to audition for the Royal School of Ballet in London where he eventually performs as a ballet dancer.

Billy's mom was not alone in understanding the power that meaningful words could have for her surviving offspring. The majority of people who responded to my survey were very clear about their desire for a legacy that preserved the loving words of their parents so that, in their absence, these special sentiments could be enjoyed over and over again. However, this isn't what we're traditionally encouraged to do. Normally, lawyers and financial advisors who give us information on preparing for the "what if" suggest that we write a Will in order to record the instructions for the distribution of our *Financial Assets*.

This is extremely important, because, if the worst does happen and you have ignored this advice, your *Financial As-*

sets will be deemed "intestate" which means that the probate court will appoint an administrator to distribute your assets according to state law. Generally the rules are pretty fair and in time your estate will be passed to your spouse, children or your next of kin. Probate is a lengthy process that can drag on for months, even years, during which time your assets are inaccessible to your surviving family, which can cause untold amounts of unnecessary stress, especially if they are unable to support themselves financially during this time. Adding insult to injury, a much higher percentage of your *Financial Assets* will also be eaten up in taxes.

Writing a Will is an essential element of preparing for the "what if," yet more as a practicality to protect your loved ones, as it fails to account for your *Total Wealth*, ignoring the immense value that exists in your *Emotional Assets*. Despite the common belief that money and material possessions are all that matter, when the life of someone dear has been lost, the value of your *Financial Assets* will depreciate rapidly. Your house, cash, company or car might appear to be the most important elements of your legacy, but in truth, these *things* will be of less significance to your survivors when your love and affection have been lost forever.

WHAT MATTERS MOST

In the course of my research I found that it is our *Emotional Assets* that matter most to our survivors. One ground-breaking study identified that the majority considered non-financial leave-behinds to be ten times more important than the financial aspects of a legacy. *The Allianz American Legacies Study* was commissioned by the Allianz Life Insurance Company and Age Wave to assess the preferences of 2,670 baby boomers (people born between 1946 and 1964) and their elderly parents, regarding the practical issues of legacies. "Many people wrongly assume the most important issue among families is money and wealth transfer, it's not," said President of Age Wave, Ken Dychtwald. He went on to say, "This national survey found that for the overwhelming majority, legacy transfer has to do with deeper, more emotional issues. An inheritance focuses primarily on the money, but a true legacy also includes memories, lessons and values you teach to your children over a lifetime."

This study was a key piece of research, providing overwhelming evidence that the desire for a legacy combining *Emotional Assets* with the more traditional aspects is in fact widespread. Although my own study was much smaller, I had obtained detailed information about people's personal preferences for a non-financial legacy. Many of the people I interviewed said they wanted a piece of memorabilia, something to keep alive the memories of their dearly departed. Some suggested it would be helpful to have a gift to open on special days, like Christmas or a birthday. One thirty year-old man, whom we'll call Matthew, said he'd like to inherit the football shirt his father had worn to the games they'd attended. Matthew believed it would remind him of the fun they'd had; helping him to recall the cheeky humor his Dad had expressed so freely during the games. Suzy, an elderly woman, wrote to say that if she could inherit one thing she'd choose her mother's apron as it would remind her of all the times happily spent cooking family meals together. Sarah, a young teenager, said she'd want the diaries her Mom had written every year since she was born, knowing that these contained the stories and secrets of both her mother's life and her own. Matthew, Suzy and Sarah's requests are very common. Although these everyday items may seem of little value, when you've lost the person you love, such seemingly unimportant things become priceless.

Despite the evidence confirming this universal desire for *Emotional Assets*, I have only encountered a few who received such a loving legacy or were thoughtful enough to create one. Yet it seems that the propensity to gift our values, rather than our valuables, is increasing. Journalist Lizette Alvarez observes this trend in her 2005 *New York Times* article, *Farewell with Love and Instructions*: "Hoping to nurture their children from afar and assuage the dread of leaving a child too soon, a small but growing number of terminally ill parents are painstakingly leaving behind more tangible links: audiotapes, videos, letters, cards and gifts that children can use to bolster memories and use as a guiding hand. The tapes bear messages of love and remembrance: the dress a daughter wore on her first day of kindergarten, the thrill of a trip to Yankee Stadium, a son's jitters before a first piano recital. The letters riff on parents' life stories, their hopes for their children and the life lessons they wish to impart. Some parents choose gifts or cards for future birthdays or Christmas celebrations. One mother created a tape to be given to her son on his wedding day, if and when that occasion arrives. One father left written messages behind paintings, a surprise that his children stumbled across a year after his death. Through these things, dying parents bequeath courage, laughter, a semblance of companionship and even a guiding hand. The keepsakes help crowd out the searing tableaux of death with reminders of how Mom or Dad sounded, moved and thought about life …"

When I first read this article, my immediate reaction was delight. "Brilliant!" I thought, "People *are* doing this and making a difference." But then I wondered, "Why hadn't Mom done this?" She was proactive, imaginative, open minded, loving, and cared about us deeply. She had all the qualities of someone who'd be inspired to leave a Legacy of Love. After giving this considerable thought, I came to the conclusion that various factors were at play. Mom had no awareness of *Emotional Assets* or the inherent value these would have for her children. No one had explained how powerful this would be, and there were no books or articles describing the long-term benefits of such a thing. I'm sure she gave some thought to sharing her stories or writing a letter to convey a loving message, but I know how scared she was of acknowledging that "it" was lurking just around the corner, and this prevented her from taking action. According to Dr. William Breitbart, Chief of Psychiatry at New York's Memorial Sloan Kettering Cancer

Center, this reaction is quite common. Commenting in Lizette Alvarez's *New York Times* article, he explains, "It's profoundly beneficial for the kids. But it is rare. Almost everyone thinks about it, but it will get delayed or put off. I think it's very difficult to do this because it really demands a confrontation, an admission, a real admission that you are dying, and that is very hard for most people. What is at play is this struggle in their mind between hope and despair. It takes on such incredible significance, a final message, it has to be said perfectly."

PRESERVING THE CONNECTION

But there are no perfect words to share when someone has passed away, just as there is no one-size-fits-all formula for creating *Your Legacy of Love*. The general themes already mentioned—your stories, values and memories, your guidance and support—will be of significant benefit to anyone surviving a loss, especially to younger children, including nieces, nephews and grandchildren, who will benefit from your wisdom regarding key life issues such as religion, relationships, growing up, sexuality, career, education and love.

The film *My Life* is a great illustration of how to go about passing on this knowledge. Made in the early '90s, this film portrays the story of happily married couple Bob (Michael Keaton) and Gail (Nicole Kidman) who are expecting their first child, when sadly they discover that Bob has cancer and may have only four months to live. Consequently they must face the fact that Bob may never meet his own son. In light of this news, Bob decides to make a film about his life with the aim of teaching his son everything that a parent should.

He begins by sharing the details of his ancestry, filming a collection of family memorabilia (including his own baby pictures), a painting of his tiny infant footprints and family photos, then he interviews friends and colleagues who share anecdotes about the kind of man he is. Bob then films himself conducting the all-important "how-to" aspects of a man's life—cooking spaghetti, playing basketball, shaving, entering a room, giving a good handshake and jump-starting a car! Finally, in an attempt to create the scenario of a father-to-son chat, Bob faces the camera and talks to his son about sex and music, explaining, "Your mother would be little help on these subjects. There are some things that have to be told straight, man to man." Bob then relays the story of how he and Gail met and fell in love, explaining that one day Gail might meet another man, possibly even remarry. Concluding his parting gift, Bob shares some selfless advice on this matter by gently advising his son that this might make him feel very angry or possibly, if he likes the new man, leave him feeling that he is being disloyal. On this delicate subject, Bob tells his son, "I will not be jealous. It will make me very happy for Gail to meet another man. I will always be your real father, and I will live on through you. I love you." The film is kept in a safe place, until the time comes when their son is old enough to understand and Gail can deliver the precious gift to him. The *My Life* scenario shows how little more than a good dose of imagination is required to capture your *Emotional Assets* and share them through *Your Legacy of Love*. This film also touches on some of the issues your survivors might encounter, giving a good example of how to deal with the idea of being "replaced" as a lover, spouse, or parent. Although this may make you rather uncomfortable, it's important to realize that such issues will affect your loved ones and that by recording your thoughts and views on these subjects, you can help clear things up in advance so your survivors aren't left wondering and worrying for the rest of their lives. Although its important to keep in mind that what you say in *Your Legacy of Love* could have a negative effect on survivors —especially young ones—and to remember that this is not an exercise in blackmail from the beyond!

THE BONUS: YOU GET PEACE OF MIND

As you embark on this journey of creating *Your Legacy of Love*, you'll soon discover why therapists have been supporting the idea of a more meaningful legacy for quite some time. Research has shown that when patients share their emotions or leave meaningful objects through what is often referred to as a "Heart Will" or "Dignity Therapy," that it makes a significant difference to their mental and emotional well-being. In recent years these concepts have generated considerable interest and support among the care community, resulting in an international clinical study into "Dignity Therapy." Led by Dr. Harvey Chochinov, director of the Manitoba Palliative Care Research Unit, this trial focused on one hundred terminally ill patients who were interviewed by a therapist:

"Tell me a little about your life history, particularly the parts you either remember most or things that were most important."

These often highly emotional discussions were recorded, capturing the information so that it could later be shared with the patients' family members and friends. Participants were encouraged to find an appropriate ending that conveyed a poignant message to their loved ones. One participant, a thirty-six-year-old woman with breast cancer noted, "I'm very happy to have participated in this project. It's helped bring my memories, thoughts, and feelings into perspective, instead of all jumbled emotions running through my head. The most important thing has been that I'm able to leave a sort of 'insight' of myself for my husband, and children, and all my family, and friends." The results of this study, which were published in the *Journal of Clinical Oncology*, showed significant benefits for both patients and their families:

91% reported a satisfaction with "Dignity Therapy"
81% felt it had or would be of help to their family
67% said it gave their life meaning

Dr. Chochinov remarked on the positive influence "Dignity Therapy" could have in significantly reducing suffering and depression for people preparing for the end-of-life. "It is noteworthy that patients who felt that the intervention had or might have some benefit for their family were most likely to report a heightened sense of meaning and purpose, along with a lessening of suffering. For dying patients, the salutary effects of safeguarding the well-being of those they are about to leave behind seems to extend to the end-of-life itself." Yet even with the promise of such a positive outcome, the idea of creating *Your Legacy of Love* might still be rather daunting. According to Dr. Donna Schuurman, Director of the Dougy Center for Grieving Children and Families, that is because, "In our largely death-denying society we have a culture that values 'moving on' rather than 'remembering'. People just don't know how to do it."

This concept is still relatively new for everyone, so it's common to be unsure and a little afraid at this stage. Whether you are the picture of perfect health, or facing your worst nightmare (with only a little time to spare), preparing *Your Legacy of Love* might appear a little challenging. I imagine that Billy's mother shed more than a few tears when penning that heartfelt letter, and the chances are you will too. Realizing your *Emotional Assets* certainly requires courage, determination and a good dose of imagination. But, remember, the gift of your love has numerous benefits for you, your surviving family, their family and the generations who are still to come. They are relying on you to help them in their time of need, to leave a reminder of who you were and how much you cared. You might find this exercise difficult at times, but please don't give up or let your loved ones down. No one knows when "that" time is going to come, so please take this opportunity to *Realize the Gift in Goodbye* and consider the words of Pablo Picasso: *"Only put off until tomorrow what you are willing to die having left undone."*

ABOUT GEMINI

British Grief Expert, Gemini Adams, trained with CRUSE, the UK's leading bereavement care organization after losing her own mother to cancer at a young age. She is the author of the multiple-award winning book, *Your Legacy of Love: Realize the Gift in Goodbye* and the soon to be released, *You've Lost the Love of Your Life, Now What?*

Gemini helps families and organizations to prepare for and overcome the challenges of loss through her workshops and classes, which she hosts in the US and Europe. She is a recipient of the Winston Churchill Fellowship, a practicing member of the National Federation of Spiritual Healers (MNFSH) and founder of: www.RealizetheGift.com – the web's largest directory for all end-of-life matters.

Discover more at: www.Realizethegift.com

CHAPTER 7

LEGACY OF LOVE – PART II

GETTING TO GRIPS WITH GRIEF

BY GEMINI ADAMS

You may be wondering, if your *Emotional Assets* are so valuable, why you haven't heard of them before, and why isn't everyone capturing them? There are actually a variety of reasons behind why most people aren't leaving non-financial legacies, which originate from the changes— in cultural, professional and historical attitudes—towards death and bereavement, that have occurred in the past century. Collectively, these attitudinal shifts have promoted our denial of the *D-Word* and conspired to prevent us from getting to grips with grief.

Until relatively recently, it was extremely common to pass on a non-financial legacy because of a shared a belief in the after-life, which motivated people to leave gifts that would maintain the connection between the living and their dearly departed. It was considered perfectly natural and normal to leave all manner of objects (which had some perceived traditional or religious meaning), as part of an inheritance. The Victorians gave lockets of hair, which their bereaved typically wore in a piece of jewelry, while South American tribes bequeathed bones for survivors to wear in their hair!

THE MADNESS OF THE "MUST MOVE ON" MARCH

These traditions began to change at the beginning of the twentieth century, as the advances in science and medicine began to alter people's attitudes about many things, including the existence of the afterlife. Rationalization became the order of the day. People began demanding proof as the medical field progressed in both technology and skill, together with our expectation for longevity. This meant that death—previously viewed as a natural and inevitable process—was suddenly perceived as a failure of modern medicine.

Behaviors and beliefs changed, shifting from a desire for a connection with the deceased to one an attitude of dread and disassociation. Not only amongst the general public, but also within the psychological community, who began adopting the belief that it was unhealthy for survivors to maintain links with their dearly de- parted. Therapists began claiming that this would promote delusions about the afterlife, hinder healing and prevent patients from moving on. The emphasis changed from *remembering* to *removing* as psychologists, psychiatrists, and counselors began marching to the beat of *Must Move On*. This mantra is something you may have witnessed personally when someone you love passed on. In the aftermath of this tragic event you may have been advised to "Stop crying; it will only upset everyone," or been told "Don't worry, you'll get over it soon." Alternatively, after some time passed, someone may have offered one of the classic *Must Move On* tenets, such as "It's been a year, you should have forgotten about them now," or "Come out tonight, it's time you moved on," or maybe they were callous enough to say, "Must you always talk about him or her? They aren't coming back, you know."

Although these comments may seem shocking, sadly, they are not uncommon. Just imagine how you'd feel if you received this kind of sympathy after you'd lost the person who had been central to your happiness for the past twenty, thirty, even sixty years; someone with whom you'd shared lessons, laughter, intimacy, arguments and even your deepest darkest secrets. It's hardly comforting to be told to "hurry up," "quick march" or "move along," as if you're running late for a busy commuter train. Unfortunately, this is the effect that the *Must Move On* mantra has had on our society and sadly it has spread way beyond the psychological community. The idea of wiping away the memories of your relationship to someone special seems a little strange to me, especially at a time when the bereaved naturally want to remember every little detail, to cling to the last remnants of the person who meant so much to them. You see, the problem with this modern mantra is that grief doesn't have a predetermined arrival and departure schedule like the 9:05 train from Grand Central. Although, I guess it's no great surprise when you look at our fast-paced and forward-focused world: a place where calm, time-consuming activities like reflecting and reminiscing appear to be so very old school. But, I can tell you that this "get over it" approach is not only confusing and unhealthy, it's also contrary to the real needs of the bereaved. This widespread acceptance of the *Must Move On* mantra has actually been very damaging, leaving behind many casualties with deep and painful wounds.

I know this because I have counseled many survivors, who, because of the influence of the *Must Move On* mantra, have buried or bottled up their thoughts and feelings. As a result, they experienced a lot of unnecessary pain and suffering. It's quite easy to spot them. They usually display some very obvious symptoms: they're uptight, never talk about *him* or *her* and are emotionally constipated, unable to express what they feel for fear of the mess when everything they've been withholding comes bursting out. They are often edgy and tired due to the tension that comes from restraining their feelings, which can leave them in a state of total exhaustion, barely surviving. The emotional toxicity caused by this suppression can be extremely dangerous for both the physical and mental health of the bereaved.

It was easy for me to spot these people because for many years I suffered like this too. I knew that despite having been persuaded by counselors, friends, or family members, that they *Must Move On* and forget about their departed loved ones, secretly wished they could share their memories or talk with someone who understood their sense of loss. That's why, when I gave them a little encouragement that "it's good to remember," the tears finally flowed and often I witnessed years of anguish wash away. For many, this was the first time they were able to feel that having a memory of their mom, dad, brother or sister was indeed okay.

For me, the *Must Move On* mantra began to take effect just a few months after Mom died. During the days that immediately followed her death (when it seemed acceptable to remember), I sat around with family members and friends happily reminiscing about the wonderful, funny, memorable times we'd all spent with her. Throughout the first few months there was a steady stream of well-wishers, sympathy cards and empathetic calls. Even when I returned to college to continue my studies, I found that my good friends were mostly supportive of my situation, but after a few weeks, something strange began to happen. People started calling to say, "You must stop moping and come out to play," others suggested, "Focus on your studies, it's your future, that's what's important now." These amateur psychologists thought they knew what was best; but they didn't. I wasn't even close to coming to terms with my loss. In fact, the reality and depth of losing my mother was only just beginning to sink in. I was suffering a total state of bewilderment, as my diary entry from the time shows:

I have no idea when I fell asleep last night, sometime in between the sobs I guess. I awoke this morning feeling destroyed. The hours of crying have completely drained me, I slept for 12 hours, but still I am exhausted. The pain is unbearable, I had no idea that anything could hurt this much. I don't know that I will ever feel happy and normal again.

The contradiction between my needs and the opinions of others only worsened over time. When I tried to talk openly about my feelings, people clammed up, turned on the TV, or changed the subject. Some stopped calling while others, to my great horror, pretended not to notice me when they saw me walking down the road, and some even crossed to the other side of the street! But it didn't stop there. When visiting a good friend, I noticed that some photographs of Mom they'd once proudly displayed were no longer to be seen. It all seemed very strange. I couldn't understand why people were acting as if Mom had never existed. I was young, confused and disturbed by this behavior, but I didn't know what else to do, so I went along with it. I didn't realize that these people were actually scared, embarrassed or uncertain of what to say. I had no idea that they'd been brainwashed by the *Must Move On* motto, so I did what seemed to be expected of me and joined in the façade.

THE GAPING VOID YOU WANT THEM TO AVOID

I began maintaining the pretense that all was well, even though this exhausted me. I had all of these wonderful memories, stories and moments that I'd shared with this great woman, yet I could no longer speak of them, so I retreated inside. This, of course, only left me feeling more separated, isolated and ignored than before. I had no one to share my suffering with, and nowhere to go, apart from the secret world of my diary, which seemed to be the only safe place to express my pain:

Today I sat at the back of the lecture room to avoid all the stares. Since I came back, everyone treats me differently, they look at me in strange ways and conversations are hushed when I walk by. Halfway through the lecture, the pain came rushing back. Those bitter tears welled in my eyes, and that agony flooded my heart. I wanted to scream. But I couldn't break down, not in front of them. It took all my strength but somehow I swallowed the pain, held back the tears and put my eyes to the ground. I have no recollection of what the lecturer said, but what matters is that I managed to contain myself until the end of class.

In their excellent *Grief Recovery Handbook*, John W. James and Russell Friedman describe this as "Academy Award Behavior." It's a classic outcome of the *Must Move On* approach, which leaves survivors acting as if they're okay when really they're not. When asked about their loss, the bereaved will often respond with statements designed to project a false image of recovery, such as, "I'm fine," or "Don't worry about me, it's my dad you should be concerned about." They do this so as not to burden others with their feelings, to prevent criticism or judgment, and to stop the scary emotions they are withholding from escaping. Unfortunately, this Oscar-winning behavior only increases the sense of suffering and isolation for survivors. This habit of rationalizing and reasoning emotions or shutting off feelings is dangerous, and if encouraged, can cause considerable emotional, physical and mental damage, driving the bereaved towards what I call the *Gaping Void*, or what is commonly recognized as the *Danger Zone* of grief.

Obviously, we don't want this to happen to your survivors. That's why it's important for you to understand how your family can have a healthy recovery from their grief. Rather than living by the *Must Move On* mantra, you can help them remain connected to you, and teach them how to openly express and release their feelings so they won't end up in the *Danger Zone*. Through *Your Legacy of Love* you can give them tools to help them cope with their grief, and to encourage their healing by helping them recall memories and motivating positive moods. With this continuing bond, they will naturally, in their own time, overcome their grief and slowly assimilate their loss.

For me, this natural acceptance took a lot longer than necessary. This was partly because I didn't receive any guidance from health care professionals, which left me unprepared to deal with my loss, but also because I didn't feel as though I could ask for help. Instead, I just kept quiet and soldiered on. There were many Oscar-winning performances to project the impression that I was doing okay. Really, I had just buried myself in my work and was pretended everything was fine, suppressing all the emotions of my grief. I compart-mentalized my feelings by squeezing them deep into the re-cesses of my body and mind. The only available space was in my heart, where the absence of my mother's love had left a hole—a gaping void. I blocked all thoughts of the woman who had been the center of my world for twenty-one years and eleven months. It was extremely uncomfortable, unnatu-ral even, and I now realize, totally unnecessary. As a result, I was stressed, edgy and worn out. I found a way to numb the pain by filling the void with a diet of drugs, shopping, and fake friends—it seemed to work. Everyone began con-gratulating me: "How great, you seem to be coping so well," or "Look at how quickly you have moved on!" I think for a while I even had myself fooled, except at night when the pretense melted away as I buried my tear-stained face in the comfort of my boyfriend's arms. Now, I'm a little savvier in matters relating to grief. I understand that this was not the way to integrate or recover from my loss. More to the point, I know for sure that the *Must Move On* approach doesn't work. It only encourages disassociation and denial while promoting damaging and destructive behaviors—warning signs that would scream DANGER to the trained eye.

I somehow survived in this state for almost two years, but as with all illusions, the bubble eventually had to burst; I had a meltdown. My extremely concerned family sent me off to see a grief counselor. Exhausted by the façade I'd been liv-ing, I happily complied. During the weekly hour-long ses-sions, I was rarely asked a single question about my Mom, other than when and how she died. Instead I was advised to remove all reminders of her from my life, take down pic-tures, destroy letters, remove her belongings and focus on the future—"How would I go about forming new relation-ships and develop my life and career?" The conversation was all one way. I was expected to talk, the counselor to listen. If I had nothing to say, we sat there in silence, staring blankly at each other. Leaving me wondering why I had bothered to leave work early, traveling halfway across London, just so that we could sit in silence or note my apparent progress (or lack of it), which seemed to be nothing more than a numb butt, and a deeper state of depression!

THE BADGE OF BEREAVEMENT

Once again, the *Must Move On* mantra had come to haunt me. All I really wanted was to talk to someone and share what I missed about my Mom, to tell them that I yearned for a tangible reminder of her love, and explain how difficult life seemed without her. After six months, when things hadn't improved, I decided to ditch the silent counseling sessions and started taking Prozac instead. Needless to say, the cocktail of anti-depressants and recreational drugs that I used to self-medicate probably wasn't the best solution! But it seemed to work, if only temporarily. It got me through my final year of college and I graduated with flying colors— which I must confess was the only positive result of using drugs and burying myself in work.

Then, it was time to leave the security of the college campus, my good friends, and the comforting arms of my wonderful boyfriend. This was the first major transition I had made since my loss, and it should have been the beginning of a new and exciting journey, but I was scared. Mom wasn't there to give me advice on this new phase of life. She couldn't share her wisdom, words of encouragement or faith in me—the very things I needed to help me trust that I could make it on my own. I wished she had left me some instructions, a "How-to" guide, or even better, a letter scribed with her familiar and supportive words: "Darling, it's okay, remember that I will always believe in you." I became truly conscious, perhaps for the first time, that Mom wasn't going to share in my struggles or successes, or watch her daughter grow into a woman, a wife, and one day a mother. She could no longer support me, guide me, or light the way. I felt completely lost and alone, and with this realization, I fell deeper into the *Gaping Void*. What on earth was I supposed to do? I knew I couldn't carry on this way, with my feelings all locked up, burdened by the baggage of my pent-up grief. Despite finding a job, my life remained a mess. I was always seeking to replace my mother's love, mostly with the attention of some random guy. I was drinking and taking drugs, although I did give up the Prozac, and I had thrown myself into work as a means of escape. Initially, the crazy hours I worked earned many compliments for my commitment, but as time wore on, I started struggling—I had to drag myself out of bed each day and was often late for work. I went through the motions but nothing felt real and I was barely scraping through the day. It seemed that my highly developed talent for pretending that everything was okay had landed me in a hole, and I couldn't seem to dig my way out.

By now, it was apparent to everyone that my attempts to "move on" were only taking me round in circles. I decided the only solution was to take matters into my own hands. Instead of self-medicating, I began self-educating; reading and listening to anything I could find on grief and bereavement. However, all the advice I found seemed to encourage the *Must Move On* approach, and I had already learned that this wasn't bringing me any closer to a healthy recovery. So I took some time out for reflection. My first epiphany was the realization that despite commonly being referred to as the same thing, grief and bereavement are two entirely different experiences.

While grief doesn't necessarily involve bereavement, bereavement always involves grief, because grief is a temporary emotional response to a change in circumstance, or the loss of something, whereas bereavement is permanent. Grief is actually something we experience on a regular basis whenever there is a change in our circumstances. However, the severity of our grief and the consequent impact on our mental, emotional, and physical well-being varies, according to the degree of change that has occurred, and the relative level of attachment we had to the former condition or person. For example, if we have a purse or wallet stolen, the natural response is a sense of loss, but it will probably only last for a few hours or a couple of days. When we move, or lose a home, perhaps because of a fire, flood or divorce, the resulting grief will last longer. It takes time to rebuild a sense of familiarity and security, to settle into a new place and way of life. During this grieving period we may have all sorts of inexplicable feelings; anger, sadness, apathy and depression. Inevitably, there will be a sense of longing for how things used to be, yet because the thing that we lost can be replaced, these feelings usually pass as we adjust to our new possessions or surroundings, and begin to form new experiences and memories. If only this were the case for the bereaved.

Bereavement is not a temporary experience. The loss of a living, laughing, loving human being or animal is permanent. No one can ever replace the person or pet we have lost. This can be an extremely difficult thing to accept, especially when "it" happens unexpectedly, or there wasn't a chance to say goodbye. In the early stages, the bereaved commonly find that they are on an emotional roller coaster ride, oscillating between states of feeling "normal" and feeling "destroyed," sometimes within a matter of hours. Everything in their world has changed; their regular and routine existence has been turned into a topsy-turvy mess. The scale of grief experienced by the bereaved is different for everyone, and will depend on how the loss occurred, the health and ages of the survivors, and their relationship to the person who passed on. Yet, because bereavement specifically relates to death, even after the devastating feelings of grief have faded, the sense of having lost something vital, and the effect this has on survivors, continues on. It can take many years to integrate the death of a loved one, while others never come to terms with such a life-changing event. Bereavement is unending, it becomes your identity; an unwelcome label that leaves you sticking out in a crowd.

Our collective understanding of grief and bereavement was born from the work of Swiss-born psychiatrist Dr. Elisabeth Kübler- Ross. During the '60s, Dr. Kübler Ross-interviewed patients at College of Chicago Billings Hospital who had been diagnosed with a terminal illness. Noting their emotional response to this tragic news, she found some commonalities in their experiences, which she referred to as the five stages: Denial, Anger, Bargaining, Depression and Acceptance. Because little other research had been conducted into grief or bereavement at that time, this study became known as the *Five Stages* model of grief and was quickly adopted by psychologists, counselors, nurses, the clergy and caregivers as a way of interpreting and helping people to "complete" their grieving. It wasn't until the '80s that more thorough investigations of the impacts of grief emerged, suggesting that the *Five Stages* model didn't really apply to people grieving the loss of a loved one at all.

REMEMBER ME WITH CONTINUING BONDS

The ground-breaking work of Dr. Kübler-Ross raised considerable awareness of a subject where previously there was none. However, the application of this model from terminally ill patients to the bereaved has caused an awful lot of confusion, and perhaps planted the seed for the rather damaging *Must Move On* model. Fortunately, during the early '90s a new concept surrounding the experience of bereavement emerged, challenging the previously upheld belief that "moving on" was essential. Extensive research conducted by twenty-two authors (among the most respected in their fields), concluded that the popular *Must Move On* model wasn't just breaking ties, but also hearts and lives—something that bereaved families had known for years. These findings, presented in the book *Continuing Bonds: New Understandings of Grief*, showed that despite cultural and professional objections, survivors were maintaining links or continuing bonds with their departed. Far from being in denial or some kind of pathological state—as was the common understanding—this ongoing connection provided a source of great comfort and solace, enabling the bereaved to find a healthy and natural resolution to their grief. After the introduction of this concept, the bereavement care and psychological communities began to recognize that a more comprehensive model of bereavement was needed. Dr. Gloria Horsley, renowned family therapist and National Board Member of America's leading grief support organization, Compassionate Friends, is a keen advocate of the need for *Continuing Bonds*. She speaks from personal experience, having lost her son, Scott, at the tender age of seventeen in a car accident.

Together with her daughter, Dr. Heidi Horsley, who co-hosts the radio show *Healing the Grieving Heart of America* and teaches several courses in grief and loss as an adjunct professor at Columbia University School of Social Work, they talk about their desire for an ongoing connection to Scott, even though everyone told them to "let go". "Well-meaning people told us we would eventually 'move on with our lives,' 'get over it,' or 'find closure.' These concepts were not confirming and did not make sense to us. We didn't want to 'get-over' Scott. To 'get over' him felt somehow like we were erasing him from our lives. Scott is the only son and brother we will ever have, and we don't want to eliminate our relationships with him. To deny them would be to deny an important part of ourselves. Yes, the pain has substantially decreased over the years, but our connections remain strong."

Thankfully, a major shift is now taking place in the way people are educated, informed and counseled about grief and bereavement. "Rather than cutting ties, we are now given permission and even encouraged to maintain emotional bonds," says Dr. Gloria Horsley. Still, many people are left to figure this out for themselves. It took me ten painful years to realize that what my intuition had been telling me was actually the healthier way to go about recovering from my loss. It wasn't until the tenth anniversary of Mom's death that I made the decision that ten years was too long; it was time to listen to my intuition and start a new chapter. Rather than the usual pretending, I tentatively began to share memories with friends and reminisce with family members about the times spent with Mom. It wasn't easy at first, as I had to reverse everything that I'd learned to do during those ten long years. Thankfully, my mother is now very much present in my life. Her photo sits proudly by my bed, and I love sharing stories of our time together. Although, this didn't happen overnight; it was a slow and often distressing experience, as the bonds that I had tried so very hard to bury, slowly unwound. But it certainly wasn't nearly as painful as being told to "cut all ties" and "move on."

I hope that you are now beginning to see just how important

Your Legacy of Love will be for your survivors, and how this can prevent them from being swayed by the *Must Move-On* mantra. When you leave them this *Continuing Bond*—your stories, values or morals, and an expression of your love—you keep them connected to you and the memories of the times you spent together, which will bring them great comfort in their time of distress.

ABOUT GEMINI

British Grief Expert, Gemini Adams, trained with CRUSE, the UK's leading bereavement care organization after losing her own mother to cancer at a young age. She is the author of the multiple-award winning book, *Your Legacy of Love: Realize the Gift in Goodbye* and the soon to be released, *You've Lost the Love of Your Life, Now What?*

Gemini helps families and organizations to prepare for and overcome the challenges of loss through her workshops and classes, which she hosts in the US and Europe. She is a recipient of the Winston Churchill Fellowship, a practicing member of the National Federation of Spiritual Healers (MNFSH) and founder of: www.RealizetheGift.com – the web's largest directory for all end-of-life matters.

Discover more at: www.Realizethegift.com

CHAPTER 8

LEGACY OF LOVE – PART III

LIFE CELEBRATION

BY GEMINI ADAMS

It's time to get personal. Everyone's doing it. Personal shoppers, personal trainers, personal development, personal computers and personal stylists—the list goes on. These days, almost every service or consumable is prefixed with the word that screams "individuality." We've evolved into a society that demands choice and lots of it. Not only in our financial services, computers and our department stores, but increasingly people are requesting a more personal service to celebrate the end of their life. Take the family who recently asked the owner of a busy company offering bespoke funerals for a memorial service on the eighteenth green of their father's favorite golf course—because that's where he spent every Sunday. Then there was the group who wanted to ride Harley-Davidsons down the street scattering the ashes of their beloved friend in their wake.

Interestingly, funeral homes are evolving to meet these changing tastes and will now do almost everything that wedding and party planners do. Bob Biggins, President of the National Funeral Directors Association, and owner of one such company, recently arranged a highly personalized service for Harry Ewell, a man who'd been selling ice cream for most of his life. Harry's ice cream van led the funeral procession and then after the service it was used to serve popsicles to the congregation. "If you call that over-the-top, then I guess I'm guilty," said Mr. Biggins in an interview with the *New York Times,* "but our business reflects society as a whole. Today's consumer wants things personal, specific to their lifestyle, whether it's highlighting a person's passion for golf or celebrating someone's deep devotion to knitting or needlepoint!"

I DID IT MY WAY!

The funeral will inevitably have a lasting impact on your survivors. That is why it's important that your memorial service actually reflects the real *you* and records the special contribution you have made to this world; the lives you've touched and the relationships you've formed, through blood, or love, wisdom or work. It should convey the lessons you've given and the insights you've shared, for which some will hate you and others will for- ever be grateful. All of this, every second, every minute of every day, every choice you've made constitutes your life, your special time in this world. This is the day when your achievements can be admired and you can be adored. Most of us have never considered how we wish to be remembered, let alone celebrated, but this is your life and it deserves to be honored. Many people are looking outside the normal traditions, turning their backs on churches, organ music and prescribed eulogies to find a tribute that reflects their personal preferences. Perhaps this shift has occurred because funerals that follow traditional procedure and protocol sometimes feel insensitive to the needs of the bereaved. It used to be that the clergy conducting the service had a long-standing relationship with the person who had died. Nowadays, a lot of people move away from their childhood homes and families, and many consider themselves "spiritual" rather than religious, so they don't belong to a particular faith. This can mean that funeral ceremonies are delivered by someone who has spent fewer than five minutes learning the brief background history of the person who has died. Not surprisingly, the resulting service can come off as a rather impersonal or anonymous affair. This can be extremely painful for the surviving family members—exacerbating their grief and making them feel that the final farewell was a farce. This is a real shame, because it doesn't have to be this way.

In *Funerals and How to Improve Them*, Dr. Tony Walter, author and Professor of Death Studies at the Center for Death and Society, Bath University, writes: "You do not have to have a religious service: you do not have to have hymns; you do not have to have a professional person take you to the service; you do not have to have a religious building, a hearse or an undertaker." It really is up to you. This is your one and only chance to say goodbye, so it should be done in the way that suits you—an attitude that is increasingly being welcomed, even by the traditionalists. Rabbi Kirshner of the Jewish Theological Seminary recently presided over the funeral of a boy whose schoolmates drew colorfully on the coffin as if it were a plaster cast. Rabbi Kirshner said, "Even though Jews are commonly buried in plain wooden coffins, this seemed to be a fitting tribute for such a young congregation." It seems that most religious representatives agree—as long as the personal preference doesn't conflict with religious or local laws, they will make an effort to incorporate your wishes into the funeral service.

Despite this trend, some still make no attempt to personalize or prepare their funeral arrangements—leaving the decisions to their surviving loved ones. However, as with many other end-of-life decisions, this passes a huge burden onto family and friends, especially partners or older children, as they are usually the ones who are left facing the "funeral dilemma," which can be extremely overwhelming for them, especially as they will probably be suf- fering from the shock of their loss. By taking control and customizing your plans for a funeral or *Life Celebration* ahead of time, you can create a service that meets your personal desires while also reducing the emotional burden that will otherwise befall your surviving family.

You might consider this exercise rather unappealing but I can assure you that my clients have a lot of fun planning their farewell parties. Tony Cornellier was one of them, a wonderful man who had tragically been diagnosed with cancer of the esophagus. Knowing that he had months, possibly weeks to live, he had been planning his *Life Celebration* and preparing for his departure: making a video of his *Life Story*, and creating his *Future Surprises*: writing cards, creating paintings and recording messages for his two grandsons. He left an impressive legacy but it was the preparations for his *Life Celebration* that really surprised me. Tony had hand-painted a hat-box, something for his ashes to be kept in. The exterior depicted a beautiful landscape of a willow tree growing on the side of a riverbank with a single bird flying high in the sky. Every day since his retirement from his job as a French teacher, Tony had taken a walk along that same riverbank where he would sit under the willow tree and meditate, reflecting on his life. When I asked him about the bird, he told me, "The bird would come and sit in the tree every spring, then one day it flew away and never came back."

When I talked with Tony about his plans for his *Life Celebration*, his life and what he had done to prepare, he was not sad, instead a little twinkle came into his eye. I asked him, "Tony, have you had fun preparing for this?" To which he replied with a great big grin, "You have no idea!" Tony's vision was something he'd carried throughout his life, so when it came to this event it seemed only natural that he should write the following note to his family and friends, which was included in the Order of Service at his memorial ceremony:

Dear Family and Friends,

All of you enriched my life and my understanding of life. Your support, prayers, calls, letters, cards, hugs and kisses and especially the tenderness you showed me, made me feel honored, respected, accepted and loved. As Antoine de Saint Exupéry wrote in The Little Prince... "L'essentiel est invisible pour les yeux" (What is essential is invisible to the eye) – Among my essentials are honor, respect, acceptance and love.

Thankfully yours,

Tony Cornellier
(November 1939 – September 2007)

THE BEAUTY OF BALLOONS

Like Tony, and many others, my Mom didn't want a typical funeral with everyone dressed in black or hymns that the congregation found virtually impossible to sing. She wanted the event to represent the life she'd lived and to share with us the fun she'd had. Unbeknownst to us, she had secretly planned her *Life Celebration* some time in the months before her death. The handwritten notes were left in an envelope with the instruction, "To be opened when I'm gone." They detailed everything: the music, a charity for donations, her preference for flowers, a list of invitees, the inscription for her epitaph, readings, poems and even an unusual request for helium balloons. We were surprised and somewhat relieved. We began implementing the plans at once, sending invitations according to her list of invitees, searching for the songs she had requested, visiting the funeral directors to choose a headstone and meeting with the priest to get approval for the balloons. There was so much to do!

It was, however, a welcome distraction from the overwhelming feelings of grief that were beginning to surface. To my surprise, the day of the service came around very fast. It was a bright, crisp day in early November, a week or so after Mom had passed. The gray skies of the past days had miraculously cleared and the sun streamed through the curtains—perfect weather, just as Mom would have wanted. I lay in bed for a while reflecting on the pe- culiarity of the day that was to follow. I was full of mixed emotions: excitement, sadness, apprehension and astonishment. It still hadn't sunk in that this was Mom's final farewell.

We entered a church packed with hundreds of people. Because everyone was dressed in bright colors rather than black, it really did look like a celebration. The helium balloons that Mom had requested were bobbing above the ribbons that attached them to the end of each pew; light blue ones to represent the sky, green for the earth, and a darker shade of blue for the sea. This personal touch was a vibrant addition to the rather sombre church interior. Respighi's, *The Birds* filled the air as we proceeded down the aisle. There was something surreal about the scene before me —Mom's coffin was set in the vestibule, covered with a beautiful arrangement of lilies which was illuminated by a glorious sunbeam streaming through a stained glass window—it had me fighting back the tears.

Mom had not been one for organized religion, so instead of the vicar reading the eulogy, she had requested three people give speeches to celebrate the many elements and achievements of her life. Ted Coleman, her first boss who trained her to become a journalist at the Skegness Standard, her colleague Dr. Pamela Ashurst and finally, her partner and best friend, Francis. They each shared stories and paid homage to the various identities of Mom: Andrea Adams; author and expert, Annie; aunt and sister, Totty; friend of many. These revealing insights took us on quite a journey. Momentarily we were dropped into the tragedy of our loss then we were filled with laughter as a joyous memory pulled our contorted brows into beaming grins. Mom chose three popular songs and two hymns; music that she felt had an appropriate message. "The Lord of the Dance" and "The King of Love My Shepherd Is" were cheerily sung by the congregation. But it was the words of her chosen songs, "Prepare the Way," from the musical *Godspell*, "By the Waters of Babylon" by Don Maclean, and "One More Angel in Heaven" from the musical *Joseph and the Amazing Technicolour Dreamcoat*, that really touched a nerve:

There's one less place at our table, there's one more tear in my eye….

During the reception, everyone commented on how wonderful the service had been. I overheard someone say, "I've never attended such an enjoyable funeral before!" Mom would have been proud. It seems that there had been nothing to worry about. The day proved better than any of us could have expected. Each element truly reflected the person we all loved and respected. The speeches gave depth and insight into her true essence, the flowers added color, the epitaph captured her deeply caring nature, and the balloons—well they were a touch of magic. More than one person noted that they were an unusual but delightful addition. However, it wasn't until later that we discovered the real beauty that lay in those balloons.

Mom had requested that following the service, there should be a small burial attended only by family and a couple of very close friends. As we formed a procession to leave the church, someone suggested we take the balloons with us. It seemed like a good idea, so we untied them from the pews, and took one each before trailing off behind the pallbearers like a crowd of children at a birthday party; walking, skipping and laughing to the burial ground. Not surprisingly, we received some strange looks along the way. That is just what she had wanted — for us to celebrate in her name. We felt her presence very strongly, giggling and skipping along with us every step of the way, but as we came to a stop, the mood changed and a sense of heaviness settled in as we huddled around the empty grave. The priest sensitively read the committal: "We commit this body to the ground, earth to earth, ashes to ashes, dust to dust," and at Mom's request scattered rose petals over the coffin as it was lowered into the ground. The finality of it all suddenly set in.

What a relief when Jacob released his dark blue balloon and it slowly began to rise. Following his lead, the rest of us let the ribbon slip through our fingers as we released our balloons skywards. Drifting in the breeze, one caught on a gust of wind and lodged itself in a tree while the other twenty or so balloons made their ascent heavenwards. Our eyes lifted up from the dark clay, into the backdrop of a vast and clean bright blue sky only to find it full of Mom and her dancing spirit traveling on. We were mesmerized. Our gaze fixed on those tiny little dots, until they turned into pinpricks and then slowly began to fade away. It was sublime. The vicar, despite being witness to thousands of burials, was lost for words. Later when capable of summing up the experience he just said "Oh my ... those beautiful balloons."

BALANCING BELIEFS, TRADITION AND RELIGION

On that November day, we successfully delivered Mom's *Life Celebration* according to her vision. She would have been so pleased to see us all enjoying her special day—a wonderful and momentous occasion. We were certainly grateful that she had taken the time to plan ahead, and I'm sure that had she not done so, the event would have been entirely different. Her advance planning really took the pressure off, even though we still had to do a lot of organizing in order to fulfill her wishes. The funeral directors weren't really set up to source CD's, helium balloons or rose petals, and the church wasn't equipped with an audio-visual system, so we had to source these things. Even though Mom had made personal requests for her *Life Celebration*, she still incorporated some of the more common funeral rituals and traditions. The priest did give a reading; he said prayers and gave the committal. There were flowers and cards, an Order of Service and a reception in the village hall. The priest and the funeral directors were of great help in these matters and were particularly supportive and sensitive when it came to choosing the casket and headstone, which we had engraved with the epitaph Mom requested:

Andrea Adams
(1946 – 1995)
Who Loves Her Children
Who Fought for Many
Against Injustice

She had managed to successfully balance her personal desires with the traditions of the church. This is something we should all aim to achieve, while also reflecting the traditions of our family, religion or community. Individualization is certainly important, but it's essential to respect your family's needs and give some thought to how your decisions will impact those left behind. While you might think it amusing to have Queen's hit song, "Another One Bites the Dust" played in the crematorium as your casket disappears behind the curtains, others might not share the joke!

Each religion has clearly-defined rituals for funerals, which are primarily designed to honor the dead while also helping the mourners to release the deceased and their grief. While some may find that these are impersonal or dull, these rituals often bring a sense of sacredness and a comforting aspect to the service. These timehonored traditions should be respected as they serve a powerful purpose. If you are not religious there are still options available to you. Rather than a priest or rabbi presiding over your funeral you could arrange for a celebrant or officiant to oversee the ceremony, someone who can conduct the proceedings in accordance with your "voice" but who doesn't need to include any religious references.

You might also want to give some thought to the many alternative burial options from the more common cremation and scattering of ashes, to the super-deluxe packages, which include embalming and fiberglass caskets in all manner of shapes and sizes. In some parts of the world, it is traditional for the coffin to represent the person's trade. For example, in Ghana one sculptor helps local fishermen to rest peacefully inside crab-shaped caskets! For those seeking a "sleep in the deep" there is an emerging American trend for reef burials. The urn holding the ashes is encased in concrete, with an inscription fixed to the exterior, before being lowered to the seabed. Companies offering the service refer to this as a "living memorial." Unusual yes, but not very practical, as your loved ones will have to scuba-dive down to visit your watery grave! For those seeking an environmentally friendly option, the best solution is a green burial in a biodegradable casket where your body can be reunited with the earth "as nature intended." Green burials are becoming more popular in England, perhaps in light of concerns raised by the European Union about the environmental impact of formaldehyde, a potent carcinogenic, which was the base for embalming fluid until it was banned throughout many parts of Europe in 2008. There are many alternative and environmentally friendly burial options available today.

If you want to explore these further, I suggest you take a look at the *Natural Death Company* or visit *www.naturalburial-company.com* and you will find additional suggestions in the Recommended Websites and Recommended Reading sections at the back of this book. Music is another area where balancing tradition and your vision can be a little difficult. Mom seemed to get the balance right with a couple of hymns and some modern songs. You may want something different from the traditional music; however, this is something that you must discuss with your religious representative to determine what they permit in their venue. You may, therefore, want to enquire about such things where you regularly attend a service, or talk to someone at the crematorium. Religious institutions and funeral providers are becoming more familiar with requests for contemporary music, as a report by the Co-operative Funeralcare found when researching the Top Ten pop songs, hymns and classical pieces that are used most frequently at British funerals.

The findings were publicized in the *Daily Mail* together with comments from Ian Mackie of the Co-op, who noted, "Tradition is still very much evident in favorite hymns while we have a growing number of people who feel that modern themes are entirely appropriate. Many now mix the two." The newspaper published the Top Ten chart of *Tunes to Put the Fun in Funeral*, with "My Way" (Frank Sinatra), "Wind Beneath My Wings" (Bette Midler) and "Angels" (Robbie Williams) reaching the top three slots for popular music. The Co-op has also seen a growing number of requests for live music. One of their employees, who is often called upon to sing at funerals, said, "There is something special and powerful about live music, which a recording just can't capture."

CREATING YOUR OWN VISION

Having moved into the age of personalization we all want to say, "I did it my way!" This is great, so long as our final-farewell party remains sensitive to the needs of remaining family members. Our choices need to be respectful to their traditions or religion, and should always be designed to bring comfort to surviving loved ones. So how do you go about creating a vision for your own *Life Celebration*? What is acceptable? How do you ensure it will be realized when you're gone? You can start with an idea—simple or extravagant—it doesn't really matter, as long as you reflect who you really are, while honoring the boundaries of local laws and, if you adhere to one, your religion. The cost of your requests should be a consideration, as making requests for professional singers to perform at your service might rack up the expense, whereas having a friend read your favorite poem probably won't cost anything.

One way to avoid financial concerns and ensure that your wishes will be fulfilled is to enter into a pre-need or pre-pay agreement with a specific funeral service company. Commonly this is funded by a funeral trust, annuity, or insurance policy and is typically managed by a trustee or insurance company, until the time comes when the money is required. This is beneficial because it allows you to specify your personal requests for the service and burial, while removing the financial burden that will otherwise fall on your surviving family. If this isn't something you wish to consider, you can simply write down the details of the vision for your *Life Celebration* and leave these instructions with your Will and Testament with a good friend, your lawyer or trusted family member.

Try to include personal insights or stories that will leave your survivors with a positive memory and make suggestions for songs, poems or readings that will offer comfort to the congregation. Various studies have shown that when the funeral is a negative experience, or fails to comfort, then the bereaved may experience unresolved grief or abnormal grief as a direct result. This is particularly important for children who are often kept away from the perceived "horrors" of funerals, based on an assumption that they will be scarred for life if they are exposed to death. However, this is not the case. Children who are proactively involved when someone has died will cope far better than those who are protected from the "truth." Whereas children who are shut out of the reality, told not to ask questions, or lied to, are being taught to suppress their emotions, to block the way they feel, and will ultimately find it difficult to trust the adults who have lied to them once they discover what really happened. Consequently, they are often very angry and hurt, and they may experience delayed grief, which can later manifest in a variety of destructive ways.

It is much healthier to explain the "whats" and "whys" of funerals to any surviving children, or grandchildren, and to do what you can to involve them. Depending on their age, you could ask them to draw a picture for you so that you can take it to heaven. You could invite them to bring a teddybear to accompany you on this journey or ask them to carry a balloon or flowers to release or place by your graveside. If you can, talk with them in advance about Life and Death issues—you will be surprised at how open most children are on these subjects. Above all, be honest with them. Explain what the event is about and give them the choice, don't make it for them.

This actually applies to everyone. Sensitivity to the needs of your surviving loved ones is essential. It will help if you can involve them in your personal vision. You can do this by holding a family meeting to discuss your preferences or simply by asking your loved ones for their opinion. By opening these subjects up to debate, you help to dissolve fears surrounding the *D-Word*. So grab a notebook (and maybe a glass of wine) to begin planning your *Life Celebration*—the event that will commemorate your incredible life, guaranteeing that you are not forgotten!

You can use the following questions as a guide to help decide what is right for this special day:-

- *The Burial*: How do you want to be laid to rest?

Buried? Cremated? Scattered at sea? What would you prefer to be buried in, an environmentally-friendly willow casket, a hand-designed fiberglass coffin, or maybe a hat-box? Where do you want the ceremony to be held? At your church, the crematorium, synagogue or temple? Perhaps in a woodland, or even on your own private property?

- *Rituals & Religion*: What traditions are essential to you and your family? What rituals will you incorporate that are specific to your religion? What meaningful additions would you like to include?
- *Music*: What message do you want to convey? Do you want traditional music, or something modern, recorded or a recital? How can you incorporate something that will motivate their mood to help your loved ones heal or leave them with wonderful *Musical Memories*?
- *Tributes & Memorials*: Is there a cause to which you would like financial donations paid? Will you accept floral tributes or is your preference for something more permanent, like a tree, a memorial bench, or memorial website?
- *Readings & Eulogies*: Who will tell the best stories of your life? Do you want them read in person or would you like to pre-record your own message and have it broadcast on the day?
- *Offerings*: Flowers, candles, incense, prayers, pictures, flags, butterflies, doves or balloons—are any of these significant to you, and do you want them used at the service?

ABOUT GEMINI

British Grief Expert, Gemini Adams, trained with CRUSE, the UK's leading bereavement care organization after losing her own mother to cancer at a young age. She is the author of the multiple-award winning book, *Your Legacy of Love: Realize the Gift in Goodbye* and the soon to be released, *You've Lost the Love of Your Life, Now What?*

Gemini helps families and organizations to prepare for and overcome the challenges of loss through her workshops and classes, which she hosts in the US and Europe. She is a recipient of the Winston Churchill Fellowship, a practicing member of the National Federation of Spiritual Healers (MNFSH) and founder of: www.RealizetheGift.com – the web's largest directory for all end-of-life matters.

Discover more at: www.Realizethegift.com

CHAPTER 9

BELIEVE – THE LEGACY YOU LEAVE LASTS FOREVER

BY JUDY ROSS, ESQ.

L auren loved her grandpa! And, in many ways, she became the apple of his eye. Over the course of their nine-year relationship, they developed a bond that surprised me as much as it gave me pause. I may have even been just a little envious, to be completely honest, because Lauren brought out something in her grandpa that few of us had ever seen. You see, my father was a man of few words. He rarely spoke of personal things to anyone, not his wife, not his children, not his friends.

Dad was a successful man, well-liked and respected. He was a wildly prosperous dentist with hundreds of loyal patients. No one ever questioned his work ethic. In fact, he was almost obsessed with work, coming from a background of little means. He had put himself through college, worked a 40-hour-week at night while attending dental school all day. Then he started his own practice right out of school.

A great provider, he had little time and even less inclination for closeness. He made a point of taking us kids to church on the occasional Sunday and on holidays, but not once did he engage us in conversations about God, spirituality, or the wonders of the universe. He definitely had a message, but it centered upon self-sufficiency: educate yourselves, never shy away from hard work, and without fail be financially responsible.

Dad was smart – very smart, actually - but he didn't waste time philosophizing about life. He always had an answer to the problems we might encounter from day to day, but his answers were short and to the point. He never used three words when two would do. You could count on logic and hard, cold facts coloring whatever conversation you might pry out of him. None of that esoteric mumbo jumbo for my dad!

Once I left home and moved on to pursue my own goals – a law career, writing, starting a business - I was more or less gone in Dad's eyes. He'd done his job; I was out in the real world and chasing whatever dreams I might have. I don't remember him ever picking up the phone and calling to see how I was doing or just to catch up. It was up to Mom to ask how school was or who the new boyfriend might be. It was Mom who asked the parental questions, like, "Are you happy?" or, "Is there anything we can do for you?"

It just wasn't in Dad's nature to get too personal; or so we all thought. Then along came Lauren, the granddaughter he was suddenly doting on at every turn. They were stuck to each other like glue, right from the start. When Lauren was a baby, she would always stop fussing the second Grandpa picked her up. When she was a toddler, she did whatever grandpa did. If grandpa worked in the yard, Lauren worked at his side. If grandpa ate lunch, Lauren ate right next to him. If we drove in the car, Grandpa and Lauren shared the backseat. When we paid my parents a visit at their home in Colorado, Lauren made sure that Grandpa had no plans other than spending time with her.

My hard-as-nails dad was like putty in Lauren's hands. He would call at least once a week to see how she was, to find out how school was going, even to get the latest news about her best friends. Lauren's happiness was vastly important to him, and she only knew him as a source of fun, happiness, advice, and support. Anytime she needed an answer to one of life's many puzzles, she called grandpa. Grandpa knew everything.

As for me, I just enjoyed seeing Dad soften up a little. It was a side of him his kids had never really experienced before. It was wonderful. Yes, he did talk to Lauren about the basics, like the importance of getting good grades, the value of saving her allowance, and being responsible, just like he had me, but now his advice had a gentleness to it. These weren't marching orders; these were words of wisdom from a grandpa.

Then the story took a serious turn. My father was diagnosed with heart trouble. We were all shocked; after all, nothing could happen to Dad. He was the one with all the answers. He was our rock. In the beginning, his doctors insisted that if he changed his diet and stuck to his meds, he'd get better. But he didn't get better. He needed surgery. Okay, so heart surgery in this day and age had a high probability of success. No problem, Dad told us. This was a relatively minor procedure, he said. No problem, we thought.

Before the surgery, all Dad talked about was the recovery

period and how long and monotonous that would be. What would he do, laying around the house all day? Lauren had the answer. She said she would call him every day to cheer him up and draw him lots of pictures for his wall. "Okay, then," Grandpa said to her. "It's a deal."

The day of the surgery we all stood around Dad's bed trying to keep his spirits up and cracking jokes about how grumpy we expected him to be once he got back home. Dad laughed. But as they wheeled him toward the operating room, he started crying. We were stunned. We had never seen Dad cry before. Did he know something we didn't?

Turns out, Dad did know something we didn't. Just before his surgery was scheduled to begin, his surgeon came to the waiting room and warned us that this was one of the riskiest procedures he had ever done. He must have seen the confusion on our faces, because he said, "Didn't your dad tell you?"

"No, he didn't," I admitted. "He called it minor heart surgery. He said the procedure had a 99% success ratio."

"I'm sorry, but that's not the case. He must have been trying to protect you," the doctor said, assuring us that he would do his best.

Halfway through the procedure, a nurse came out. "Your dad's okay. He's on the heart bypass machine."

Then she came out again. "He's doing alright. He's off the heart bypass machine."

Then one of the surgical team came out. "Your father's heart is in very bad shape. We're doing the best we can. He's fighting for his life. The one thing he has going for him now is the skill of his surgeon. He's one of the best."

Dad did make it through the surgery. But two hours later, he was back in the operating room. He made it through that too. However, days passed before his eyes opened again. When they did, we were ecstatic. And so thankful to have more time with him!

As it turned out, the time was short and more trying than I could have ever imagined. Dad was in the hospital for two months and in and out of ICU the entire time. On and off the respirator. Finally, his doctors said they had to do a tracheotomy; and then Dad would be sent to a nursing home. He refused. He said he didn't want to live that way. He just wanted to be taken off the respirator and allowed to die naturally.

During those two months in the hospital, we didn't ask Dad any of those "important life lesson" questions. We all believed he would recover and come home; we had years to ask him those questions. Then suddenly we were called back to the hospital. "Be prepared to say your goodbyes," we were told.

One of the hardest things I ever had to do was to tell Lauren we needed to fly back to Colorado to see Grandpa, probably for the last time. She was nine at the time. Grandpa was her best friend. With tears streaming down her face, she asked, "Who will answer all our questions if Grandpa's not here anymore?" It broke my heart. Why hadn't I asked Dad to record some of his thoughts for Lauren? Why hadn't I given him a tape recorder to leave her the sound of his voice and to share some of his pearls of wisdom? Why hadn't I considered how much these things would have added to his legacy, and how much they would have meant to his granddaughter?

The whole family gathered in his room that day.

My dad had always loved a good glass of wine, so when they took him off the ventilator one last time, we all shared a bottle of his favorite – a Pinot Noir from a special winery in Napa – and toasted to his life. The emotions were so strong and the time was so short that I didn't think to ask him any of those "important life lesson" questions. I was just so glad to be in the room with him.

He held on all through the night and we stayed with him. Before he passed away, he motioned for his granddaughter to come close. Lauren stepped up to him. She leaned over the bed, and he whispered to her one last word. "Believe."

Believe? That one single word! What had he meant? Did he mean believe in God? Believe in the goodness of others? Believe in yourself? Believe in your abilities? What did he mean???

"Believe" was not a word my father used, not as a way of motivating us or instructing us, and not as a matter of faith or guidance. I couldn't recall a single time he had ever used that term. And yet it was his last word to her. What was he trying to tell my daughter?

The question still haunts me. I would love to know exactly what he meant. For Lauren, it's different; she doesn't question it. It was the only guidance her grandfather left her so she's making the most of it. "Believe" is her mantra when she plays tennis. It's her guide. She's even etched "Believe" onto the heels of her tennis shoes and keeps a picture of her grandpa in her shoe during tournaments.

But there is another side to this single-word legacy, and that's the fact that is *just* a single word when it could have been so much more. Lauren really misses her grandpa's love, and there are plenty of times when she longs for his counsel. How many times have I heard her asked, "What would grandpa say?"

Every time she does, I realize how nice it would be to have a recording of grandpa expressing some of those pearls of wisdom or a journal of some of his inner most thoughts. We did look. We searched through his private papers for anything he might have left behind, but there was nothing more than a simple will. No customized thorough estate plan, no notes, no journal, and certainly no recorded messages.

Oh, how I wish his estate planning attorney had encouraged Dad to do more; imagine if he had left behind a recorded legacy conversation. This "missing piece" is one of the primary reasons why I decided to become an estate planning attorney; I didn't want other families to go through what my family had gone through, wishing there was more for all of us, but especially for Lauren.

Legacy planning is about passing on who you are and what's important to you, and encouraging my clients to do just that has become an integral part of my practice.

Here are three simple rules-of-thumb that I share with my clients when it comes time to prepare a legacy plan:

1. A recording is often preferable to a journal or filming. A recording doesn't require attention to grammar or word usage; there are no lights or cameras to make you uncomfortable. It's simply a loved one talking in a conversational voice, sharing, remembering, elucidating. Before I became an estate planning attorney, I kept telling myself to write something down for my daughter in the event anything ever happened to me. But I never got around to it. It was too difficult. Then I participated in a recorded legacy conversation and discovered how easy and how personal it was to express myself

verbally. Now I have a CD that I know Lauren will listen to and treasure when I'm gone.

2. Make your recording *after* you've signed all of the important asset transfer documents for your estate plan. With that often-stressful task out of the way, you can concentrate on a life message that comes purely from your heart and soul.

3. Finally, I encourage you to record your legacy message with the aide of your trusted attorney, someone who is trained to guide you through the process, and to illicit thoughts and stories you might otherwise have forgotten or failed to expand upon. I know that the more relaxed and natural my clients feel, the easier it is for them to engage in a meaningful conversation about important topics that can comfort their loved ones for many generations to come.

I know that Lauren wishes her grandpa had made such a legacy recording. Imagine the impact his words would have on her as she travels through her teenage years and into adulthood. Yes, she has her memories, and she will always treasure those memories. However, the sound of a loved ones voice sharing his or her most intimate and meaningful thoughts lives forever.

ABOUT JUDY

Judy Ross is a Personal Family Lawyer with the Family Wealth Planning Institute. Her practice focuses on the creation of life-long relationships with her clients. Her goal is to offer advice and counsel as her clients' lives evolve, their assets grow, and the law affecting those assets changes. As a parent, Judy understands the importance of protecting your family while focusing on who you are and what's important to you.

Judy's passion for helping people is what attracted her to the area of estate planning, and she provides diligent legal services to her clients with pride, integrity, and compassion. Just as importantly, she understands the value of leaving behind a legacy that makes family and friends proud. That is why she founded the Ross Legal Group. And that is why she is so dedicated to easing the burden of individuals and families making complicated legal decisions to ensure their well-being and the well-being of their loved ones.

Judy is a member of WealthCounsel, LLC., which allows her to collaborate with top attorneys and financial professionals nationwide on advanced estate planning strategies. Most importantly, it affords her the opportunity to give her clients the individualized personal attention conducive to a small firm while staying on the leading edge of estate planning knowledge. She is also a member of the Orange County Bar Association – Trusts & Estates Law Section, and the San Diego County Bar Association – Estate Planning, Trust & Probate Law Section.

Judy earned her Juris Doctorate degree from Western State University School of Law (Fullerton) in 1998 and her Master's of Law in International Taxation with a concentration in E-Commerce Law (LL.M Intl. Tax) from St. Thomas University School of Law (Miami) in 2004. She is admitted to practice before the California Supreme Court and the United States District Court for the Central District of California.

Judy Ross is much more than one of Orange County's outstanding estate planning attorneys, she is a dedicated mother and friend. She has authored two wonderful children's books and believes in the power of family and community. She loves playing tennis, even though her 14-year-old daughter now beats her on a regular basis!

Judy resides in Orange County, California with her family and their dog Loppy.

CHAPTER 10

PUT YOUR HOUSE IN ORDER

BY MEG OBENAUF, ESQ.

At 6:37 a.m. on August 1, 2008, I was sitting on the couch reading to my one-year-old son when my water broke. Under normal circumstances this is an exhilarating, slightly scary event. The problem? These were not normal circumstances—my baby was not due for another 8 ½ weeks.

I was terrified.

Since the doctor's office was closed, I called my HMO's dial-a-nurse, and within four minutes, she told me what I already knew—I had to get to the hospital.

This definitely was not in our plan. I was at home alone with my son—my husband already was at work. I had no bag packed. And I had no childcare—my parents were not scheduled to arrive for weeks.

I called my husband to come home right away. Irrationally, I compensated for my lack of planning by filling a huge cooler with food for my son. I suppose I was thinking that wherever he ended up, at least he would be well fed. I packed clothes, toys and diapers. I had no idea what I would do with him. I called the mom hosting our playgroup that day, and my call went straight to voicemail.

After I cleaned up and threw some t-shirts and underwear for myself on the bed, Mark arrived home, found me a suitcase, and we headed down the volcano to the hospital. We are fortunate to live on Maui, Hawaii. However, we do not have all the hospital facilities residents require, and I knew that Maui did not have a Neonatal Intensive Care Unit (NICU).

Both my husband and I are from Illinois, and all our family lives on the U.S. mainland. We have lived on Maui for over 12 years and have developed a great group of friends. However, I was not thinking clearly and could not determine who would be available at 7 a.m. on a weekday. I still was hoping we only would need a limited amount of childcare, and that the doctors would have some medication for me that could stave off labor for a week or so, to allow our baby a little more time to grow.

As we drove, Mark called his best friend, who happened to be off work. Although not a father or frequent babysitter, our son loves "Uncle" Dave. Dave agreed to watch Cooper if needed. I wasn't sure if Dave even knew how to change a diaper, but I figured our son could talk him through it.

At the hospital, we got as far as the Labor and Delivery lobby when security stopped us. Unlike many more progressive hospitals, our hospital does not allow children in Labor and Delivery. Mark and Cooper had to wait outside. I went in alone.

The next hours alternated between urgent immediacy and long stretches of waiting. The doctor, 1-1/2 hours past the end of her shift, consulted by telephone with the perinatalogist on Oahu who had seen me each week on Maui. I tried to overhear their conversations to determine which way they were leaning—transport to Oahu or delivery on Maui. I sneaked cell phone calls to Mark from my hospital bed to the waiting area.

All alone, I had to make critical decisions about myself and the baby without input from my husband. I knew the medical team would decide where our daughter would be born based on her best interests, but I begged them to fly us to Oahu. I desperately wanted her to be born in a hospital with a NICU. The alternative would have been our daughter, immediately after birth, flying solo to the Oahu hospital. My husband could have taken the first available commercial flight to meet her there, but I would not be able to see her until after I was released from the hospital, which after a C-section, would likely have been days later.

I couldn't stand the thought of our new baby alone on that airplane.

My contractions were five minutes apart, but because I was only 1 centimeter dilated, the medical team allowed me to fly as long as my blood pressure decreased. The team began preparing me for transport, and I focused on deep breaths.

Dave soon arrived to take care of Cooper. As luck would have it, my nurse was semi-retired, only worked one day a week, and did not feel particularly beholden to hospital rules. She helped Mark sneak our son into my room so I could say goodbye. He knew my doctor from my prenatal visits and was really excited about mommy and daddy flying on a plane to see Dr. O while he spent the day with Uncle Dave.

With Cooper in good hands, Mark stayed with me while we awaited the plane's arrival from Oahu. I expected we would travel to the airport to meet the airplane. What actually happened is when the airplane arrived, the air ambulance crew hailed a commercial taxi from the airport to the hospital!

Finally, the two air crew members arrived at the hospital and reviewed my file. Because of the intravenous magnesium sulfate I'd been given, my contractions were down to seven minutes apart. The team called an ambulance, and we FINALLY were under way.

Sharing our airport gate was a giant Coast Guard airplane creating a mind-numbing amount of noise. Before disembarking from the ambulance, the EMTs placed sunglasses and headphones on me, and we rolled out into the bright sunshine and deafening noise. Everyone wore headsets except Mark. It felt like some kind of war zone.

On the plane, things started happening very quickly. My contractions came faster and faster. They accelerated to two minutes apart. The medics gave me some kind of 'shot' which briefly extended them to three minutes apart.

Mark was on the plane with me, but I could not see or hear him (I'm pretty sure he could hear me, however). The medics strapped me to a gurney on my side. The female EMT was kind and supportive. I remember worrying I would crush her delicate hands, so mostly I sort of clawed at the leather seat opposite me. The team kept in frequent contact with the Oahu hospital about my condition. Over the noise of the plane (and well, me), I overheard the EMT reporting "She's pre-positioning!" and even, "She's Dr. Jekyll and Mr. Hyde!"

I tried to remember the breathing exercises from my child-birth class two years before. Mostly I just prayed fervently for our daughter to hold on a little longer. I knew it would be terrible for her to arrive on the plane, primarily because I had been told I needed to have a C-section, which obviously they cannot perform on a plane. In hindsight, I know my placenta was abrupting and they would not have been able to help my daughter in the way she needed on that plane.

At the peak of my contractions, when the pain was the worst, I reminded myself that the team had promised me I would be going right into surgery upon our arrival at the hospital. I envisioned a nice man waiting for me with a big needle. Mostly, I prayed.

After our landing on Oahu, the ambulance could not reach the airport gate, because someone had changed the lock. Again we waited. Finally, the ambulance reached us, and we raced to the hospital.

I remember vividly my relief when the elevator doors opened into the hospital. We may have been in the basement corridor, but we were in the hospital, and I knew we were going to be okay.

The doctors called a neonatal "code" when we arrived, so when we reached Labor and Delivery, it seemed as though every doctor and nurse in the hospital was in that room. There was not time for a C-Section or, for that matter, pain medication. The doctor told me not to push, and we waited for the NICU team to arrive.

The minute the NICU team ran into the room with a crash cart, everything changed. The nurses yelled, "PUSH! PUSH!", and I did. In addition to the NICU team, there were two nurses on my sides and two doctors at the end of the bed with Mark, the EMTs behind the nurses and various other people running around the room.

When the medical team lost our baby's heartbeat on the fetal monitor, the doctor told me she HAD to come out on the next push. And, seven minutes after crossing the threshold of the hospital, she did.

Kalia was "depressed", which means not breathing or moving but with a heartbeat. The nurse practitioner resuscitated her, and Kalia responded within one minute, preventing them from having to insert a breathing tube. Kalia's APGAR score at one minute after birth was 1 out of 10. Her five-minute APGAR was 6, and her 10-minute APGAR was 9. The nurse practitioner told me she did not worry much about neurological issues for babies with five-minute APGARs over 5, and this caused me great relief.

Kalia was a "rock star" in the NICU. She was off all machines and oxygen by the next day and quickly became a "feeder-grower".

Meanwhile, back on Maui, Uncle Dave and Cooper had a great day, and Dave dropped our son off at his wonderful childcare provider's home for the night. Cooper was used to eating and sleeping there, so it was a comfortable fit for him. Mark flew home to Maui, and for the next several weeks, I remained on Oahu with Kalia, while Cooper flew back and forth each week with my parents.

Nineteen days after her arrival, we flew home to Maui on August 20, 2008. Kalia was up to 3 pounds, 11 ounces. She thrived. She was discharged from early intervention services at one year and has continued to amaze us.

Months later, when I finally came up for air and my attorney brain started working again, I realized exactly how lucky we were, not only from the obvious medical standpoint but from a legal perspective as well. Neither of our son's care providers that first weekend had any legal authority whatsoever to care for him. If he had hurt himself or become ill, they would not have been able to authorize medical treatment for him. I am sure Mark was not answering his cellular telephone after we left Maui, and I didn't even know where my phone was once we boarded the plane.

I also couldn't help but wonder if this had been a different kind of medical emergency—where Mark and I were the patients--what would have happened with the children. I am an attorney, and I had an estate plan and had nominated guardians for our children. However, in a classic "physician heal thyself" scenario, my health care directive and all my husband's documents were lying unsigned in a pile of paperwork on our desk, where they had been sitting for months.

Although I had nominated long-term guardians for our children, all our choices live on the mainland and have their own families. I know if necessary they would come as quickly as possible, but I did not know if that would be the next day, in two days, or a week. In the meantime, no one had the legal authority to care for or authorize treatment for our children. Who would be making decisions for our daughter in the NICU or authorizing treatment if something happened to our son?

The truth is that the authorities may very well have had to take them into protective custody. When no one can give consent to medical treatment for children, the state steps in to take authority over the children. In my area, this works by the police taking "protective custody" of children. The police are met at the hospital by a Child Welfare Services worker, who finds a foster placement for the children. Often, our CWS workers try to find a family member they can "special license" to care for the children.

In our case, we have no family members on our island. I realized that it is entirely possible that, on this hypothetical worst of all days for our children, they could be in the care of strangers until their guardians arrived from the mainland.

Is this a preventable problem? Absolutely, and I knew I had to get the word out. With three simple steps, parents can prevent their children from having to be out of the hands of their chosen caregivers for even a moment.

The first step is to nominate temporary guardians for your children. These first responders should reside within twenty minutes of your home. They do not need to be the people you have nominated for long-term guardians. The first responders should be people your children know well and with whom they feel comfortable.

Step Two is to give the temporary guardians the legal authority they need to make medical and legal decisions for your children until the long-term guardians arrive. The temporary guardians can present this document to a police officer or doctor to authorize them to make critical decisions for your children.

Finally, carry a card in your wallet listing the temporary guardians in the order you want them contacted with their cell phone numbers. I keep mine right behind my driver's license. Give emergency personnel the information they need to make the best decisions for your children.

I was so surprised that with all my legal training, I had neglected to plan thoroughly for the most important people in my life! And I was far from alone—a huge percentage of parents have not named guardians for their children at all, and most of those who have named long-term guardians have not given first responders proper authority.

I have seen the air ambulance many times in the sky over Maui, but believe me, I never thought I would be the one riding on it. Follow the three simple steps above, and you can rest assured that in the worst-case scenario, your children will remain with people you have chosen who love and cherish them.

ABOUT MEG

Meg Obenauf is a lawyer-mama living in beautiful Maui, Hawaii. As the founder of Obenauf Law Group, Meg strives to help families pass on their wealth simply, without conflict, drama, or taxes. Meg helps parents of minor children create plans so that their *keiki* are never out of the hands of their loved ones, even for a moment, if the unthinkable should occur. She works with clients to create customized plans designed to ensure that their wishes are recognized and followed.

Working with Meg means that your estate plan will encompass not only asset preservation and continuity, but also the non-financial stories and wisdom you wish to pass along.

Meg recognizes the importance of incentivizing her clients to keep in touch with her, so your plan works when you need it. Therefore, all estate-planning services at Obenauf Law Group are billed on a flat-fee basis with NO surprise bills or hourly rates. The team at Obenauf Law Group wants their clients not to be afraid to call and email them!

Meg is a graduate of Harvard Law School. She resides in upcountry Maui with her husband, Mark, and her two young children, Cooper and Kalia.

To learn more about Meg and the Obenauf Law Group, visit them at: www.obenauflawgroup.com or call (808) 244-3905.

CHAPTER 11

THE RISE AND RUIN OF A REAL ESTATE FORTUNE

BY PETER SAHIN, ESQ.

Norman Bradbury followed in his father Jim's footsteps and took over the family civil engineering company in 1964 after finishing his Master's Degree in Engineering. Norman had a naturally gregarious and likeable personality, a strong work ethic, and treated his clients and staff like family. Company profits grew steadily with Norman at the helm. Along the way, he took full advantage of real estate investment opportunities that came his way by virtue of his professional expertise and relationships in the community. His calculating approach and assertiveness made him well-equipped to 'jump on good deals' at just the opportune times.

In 1970, Norman purchased a distressed but well constructed 25-unit apartment complex in an 'up and coming' neighborhood and saw his insider research pay off when the property was annexed into a top school district three years later. The income from the property helped pay for a nice ring and the wedding a year later when he tied the knot with Mary, his college sweetheart. In 1974, he acquired an office building that soon saw rent and occupancy rates soar when its prime location adjacent to a proposed freeway extension became official and went public. Then in 1979, he felt only slightly guilty "stealing" six acres of industrial-zoned land at auction for pennies on the dollar thanks to his ability to submit an 'all cash' offer. Just four months later he came to terms on a twenty year lease with a detergent manufacturing company that turned that investment into his most profitable purchase. The income from his savvy investments over the years comfortably put his four kids through college and afforded him and Mary a financially secure life together.

It wouldn't be a stretch to say that Norman had the 'midas touch' when it came to real estate investing. But he also had some character traits that would ultimately ruin everything he managed to build. Early in his professional career he endured a long, expensive, and nasty lawsuit with a former employee that left him with a deep-rooted distrust of lawyers that was hard to shake. As a result, the mere thought of putting his trust in a lawyer to get his assets and affairs in order made his flesh crawl. Additionally, while Norman did a magnificent job of living life to the fullest each and every day, psychologically he never really could come to terms with his own mortality. The truth was that death really scared Norman. So much so, that whenever the topic came up, he would make selfish sounding statements like, "I don't give a hoot what happens when I'm gone." Those close to him though knew this wasn't really true. He did, however, prefer to just stick his head in the sand and ignore the issue of planning for his own death, as if that would make it go away. Norman was also a border-line 'control freak' and didn't much like the idea of giving the wheel up to others. Even after his 65th birthday, his wife practically had to threaten moving out before he reluctantly agreed to sell his share in the engineering company to his younger partner for $3 million.

It would be ten years later, late in the spring of 2006, when Norman collapsed in the backyard and had to be rushed to the emergency room. The many years of social eating and drinking had taken their toll, leaving Norman in poor health. By then he had accumulated a net worth of nearly $13 million, with most of his wealth in real estate holdings. In keeping with his controlling nature, except for the family home, most of the real estate was held in his own individual name. When he was released from the hospital four days later, he realized that he had to do something to ease Mary's anxiety and concerns. The two of them downloaded a simple living trust document online for $79 and signed the papers that day. In light of the doctor's strict 'no work' instructions, Norman reluctantly agreed that Mary should be the sole "Trustee" or manager in charge of the living trust assets. Neither really understood a whole lot more about the papers, but Mary felt better once Norman signed them and she filed the documents away in the office bureau. Over the next six months, Norman's health steadily deteriorated until he passed away in his sleep one winter night with Mary by his side.

After the memorial service, Mary took the trust papers to a lawyer recommended by a family friend of many years. The primary reason she had managed to get Norman to sign the papers was their belief that a living trust would allow the family to avoid having to go through the probate courts if anything happened to him. What she discovered at her meeting with the lawyer, however, is that just signing a trust agreement didn't alone guarantee that. What they didn't realize when they downloaded the trust document was that each of the assets they owned had to be re-titled correctly to work with their trust. However, in their case except for the family home owned jointly with Mary, all of the real estate and most of their accounts had remained in Norman's name. The problem was made worse by the fact that Norman was not named as a trustee on the documents, making a full probate unavoidable in their case despite the existence of their trust.

Mary discovered that the probate was going to cost their family over $700,000. The cost of probate would be especially hard on them as property owners because it was calculated on the total market value (total selling price) of the real estate holdings irrespective of how little equity there was in the assets. In addition to the alarming probate costs, she was 'blindsided' when she found out about their estate tax exposure. The way things were, the Bradburys were looking at over $4 million in estate taxes, leaving far less of what otherwise appeared to be a significant nest egg for their children and grandchildren.

A dark cloud hung over Mary when she thought about everything she had to manage while dealing with the loss of her now departed Norman. Having her children and friends by her side was a comfort, but she needed some time alone to grieve and process how she would carry on without Norman. She decided to drive up the coast to a small seaside village where she and Norman used to vacation together when they wanted to get away. Her children were strongly against the idea of her heading off by herself in her current condition, but they had their own families and jobs to attend to, so they reluctantly saw her off for a week away. Later that evening, Mary's eldest daughter, Jessica received a phone call at the house...her mother had been in a serious multi-vehicle accident on the coast highway. Mary did not survive the crash.

Following the sudden loss of both their parents, the children did their best to pick up the pieces. The probate case was opened and Jessica was appointed as the estate representative and took over as trustee as well. The probate court process required potential creditors of Norman and Mary's estate to be notified of the case. Within 3 months after Jessica's appointment, a major estate liability surfaced. A claim was asserted against Norman's estate by the Regional Water Quality Board and a neighboring property owner, based on his standing as the land owner of the six acre industrial site he purchased in 1979. The claim alleged environmental contamination of the local water basin due to the activities of the laundry detergent manufacturer that operated on the property for 20 years, and Norman was a responsible party by virtue of his past ownership status. Because these environmental claims were under a theory of strict legal liability, it did not matter that the activities of the industrial tenant were legal at the time they operated or that Norman had been unaware of the issues surrounding their activities. Everything the children stood to inherit was now at risk.

What ensued for Norman's four surviving children was a legal nightmare that would have kindled his own worst fears. The probate case would remain open indefinitely, while multiple parties spent hundreds of thousands of dollars in litigation over the environmental cleanup responsibilities. Between the $700,000 probate fees, the $4.1 million estate tax bill, the $7 million environmental claims, and the retained litigation attorneys, the children soon realized that the entire nest egg their parents had methodically and honesty built up over 30 years would end up in the pockets of others.

Francis Bacon coined a much repeated and often borrowed aphorism – better known today as "knowledge is power." One might expand on it to say that knowledge combined with action can be truly powerful. The really sad part about the Bradburys' story is that if Norman had known what to do and been willing to take the right actions, he could have done so much to protect his loved ones from what transpired. Ironically enough, his own fears and unwillingness to accept help, led his loved ones down a path he never would have wanted them to be forced to travel.

Had Norman sought the help of an expert with a focus on helping real estate investment owners like him, he could have kept his holdings safe and secure for future generations. In his case, a trusted advisor would have helped him plan ahead by transferring most of his holdings into a special trust, where they would be sheltered from the up to 55% estate tax affecting assets that shift between generations and from future creditor claims against his children's inheritance. An attorney who had his interests at heart would have personally helped him ensure everything he owned was properly titled to avoid court involvement for his family. Additionally, an attorney who understood the unique planning strategies for owners of potential environmentally-impacted properties would have known that Norman's best strategy for his industrial land would have been to keep it completely outside of any trust created during his lifetime, so future environmental claims and clean up obligations could proceed under legal exemptions – which would have protected his children from excessive liability exposure.

Although it is sad and tragic, we can learn something from Norman Bradbury's story and take action to not just live well in our own lives, but to also take care to protect what we've achieved for the good of future generations as well.

ABOUT PETER

Peter A. Sahin, Esq. specializes in estate planning and liability protection for individuals, families, and businesses. He focuses on developing long-term relationships with his clients, so he can help to protect them throughout all of life's changes.

Peter received his undergraduate degree from UCLA and graduated with honors in the top 5% of his class from Whittier Law School. After graduation, Peter served as staff counsel for the nation's largest privately owned insurance company and was an associate at a premier Orange County business law firm. He founded his own estate planning and business firm in 2005 with the mission of helping clients safeguard their assets, families and loved ones.

Peter prides himself on his ability to truly listen to each client's history and background in order to provide the right counseling for their specific needs. Having spent his childhood in four different countries and six U.S. states, he appreciates the unique composition of each family and knows firsthand that thoughtful, solid planning can maximize both financial and family security.

Peter resides in Orange County with his wife, Laurel, and their Boston Terriers, Humphrey and Bogart. Peter enjoys traveling, tennis, skiing, yoga, surfing, and triathlons.

CHAPTER 12

ESTATE PLANNING: MAKE IT PERSONAL

BY CHRISTINE E. FAULKNER, ESQ.

"What we've got here is a failure to communicate."

~ From the film: *"Cool Hand Luke"*

We all strive for family harmony in our lives. I remember when my own children were born – I dreamt of a beautiful family life where my kids could grow up in a peaceful and happy home. For the most part, I think we've accomplished this – but, in all honesty, like most families, we do have our days where our harmony hits a few sour notes!

For many families, however, that harmony is only skin deep – and unresolved tensions can often hit the boiling point when a loved one passes away. When everyone avoids dealing with what is truly meaningful to all parties, it can result in unfortunate and even devastating outcomes for surviving family members.

The big mistake most of us make? Proceeding as if a legacy is only about money – when it's much more complex than investments, real estate and the amount of cash left in a bank account. All families have emotional issues to face up to – and few of us realize that these intangibles can often be far more powerful than any amount of money, as well as a great deal more destructive.

In this chapter, I will discuss the vital importance of dealing within the family on these crucial issues before it's too late, so harmony and understanding can prevail over unnecessary and unpleasant conflicts. Make no mistake – many of these conflicts are often inevitable. If everyone works together with good intentions towards common goals of reconciliation, they can often be resolved amicably so that hard feelings are dissipated. By respecting traditions and sticking to core ideals, families don't have to be divided by a death – they can even end up closer than ever before.

THE CONSEQUENCES OF NOT COMMUNICATING

Experts agree that estate planning is an essential component of a comprehensive financial plan. The average American married couple, usually comprised of two parents with full time careers, works hard over their lifetimes to build their financial assets, and understandably, they want to protect those assets and pass them on to their heirs as easily as possible.

A will, a trust, an advanced health care directive and power of attorney are typically the basic estate planning documents needed to protect these families, depending in which state they reside. For example, in California, trust planning is important to protect a family from the heartache and considerable expense of probate, as well as possible exposure to estate taxes. Proper trust planning also allows for control in determining *when* heirs or beneficiaries will receive property and in what manner they will receive property, according to when *we* decide, rather than when the law decides – usually at 18 years old.

More importantly, however, estate planning allows you to make important decisions about your legacy if something happens to you. This process allows all of us to contemplate our lives and what they mean to those left behind. Believe it or not, when we give real consideration to the deeper aspects of our family relationships and openly discuss those thoughts with family members, an estate plan can enable us to express our love, values and ideals in a meaningful manner after we're gone.

On the other hand, no estate plan, or a poorly thought-out one, can have potentially devastating and long-term consequences on family unity and harmony. And I'd like to share one real-life example of what can happen when an estate plan takes everyone by surprise, creates unintended conflict that tarnishes a legacy and divides the surviving family.

This true example involves a family that was a uniquely blended one – each spouse had two children from a previous marriage. Their union also produced two more children, bringing the total to six. At the time they married, the father owned a successful business; the mother stayed home to raise the children. The family did well, but they were by no means what anyone would consider wealthy. The father worked many, many hours and, when time and money allowed, he and the mother would get away together for some well-earned R&R.

The father was an avid golfer, spending much of his time off working on improving his game; he continued playing golf well into his 80s. He valued education, having built his own company with nothing more than a high school diploma and an excellent work ethic. He hoped his children would achieve as much or more than he had, and believed a college education was crucial to his kids' future success.

The mother was the glue that held the family together. She was the type of woman who got up early every morning to make breakfast for and spend time with her husband before he left for work. She raised the kids, mostly the younger four of the six (the eldest two were already teenagers), and was a livewire, spunky and energetic, quick to smile, and loved the finer things and all things feminine. Her dressing room was adorned with beautiful perfume bottles and lovely figurines, and her jewelry box was filled with necklaces, bracelets and earrings that she enjoyed wearing.

Eventually the father retired, and the youngest son took over the family business. The other kids all moved away, started their own careers and some had families of their own. The mother and father now spent time traveling and spending holidays with the kids and grandkids. The three groups of kids began to drift apart - seeing one another only for the occasional birthday or anniversary party.

As the mother and father got older, they knew they needed to plan what to do with their money and property, so they met with an estate-planning attorney and entered into what they thought was prudent estate planning. They walked away with a trust and wills, assuming everything was well taken care of.

The mother passed away a few years later from a terminal illness. The father felt lost without his beloved wife, and their children took the loss hard. The estate plan was simple enough – it provided that all property, both real and personal, would pass to the father in the event of the mother's death. It seemed the natural way to do things.

The problem came with the mother's biological children – neither parent really considered what the impact of the father inheriting all her property, some of which she owned before she married him, would be. Nothing was really discussed – but the seeds of anger and resentment were planted.

Years later, the father passed away. By that time, only four children were still living – one child the couple had together, one child from mom's first marriage and two children from father's first marriage. The estate plan had not been updated and no provision whatsoever was made to ensure that any of the mother's personal property went to the child from her first marriage. As a matter of fact, except for a few specific items, the estate plan did not specify who would inherit *any* of the personal belongings - so it was left to the surviving four children to make the decision amongst themselves.

As the children were upset and grieving, this decision-making process was very difficult. Everything in the house was very personal to the remaining kids – deep emotions and memories were very much in control. While the way they decided to divide up the deceased couple's possessions seemed reasonable at the time, it led to disastrous results.

The kids decided that the fairest way to divide the personal items was to list them all and divide them between the four so that each child received a portion of roughly equal value. Without any alternative specified in the actual estate plan, this seemed a logical way to settle the matter. Unfortunately, this approach only considered the monetary worth of the property – not the personal or emotional value that each child attributed to each item.

Many of the mother's personal items, such as the jewelry, had a lot more value than the father's. Her biological children understandably wanted what had belonged to their mother, regardless of its monetary value – unfortunately, most of the rest of the items had very little monetary worth. Disagreements broke out amongst the four.

With emotions running high, the father's oldest children went to take care of the funeral arrangements. When they returned to their parents' home, they found that valuable property was suddenly missing – and so was one of the mother's children, who never returned for the funeral. Rather than attempt to discuss the division of property any further, the child had simply taken what was important to her. It wasn't a question of money to her – it was a question of sentimental value.

One child sided with the one who took the mother's property. The other two remaining children lined up against them. To this day, neither set of children has again spoken to the other – their family relationship was irreparably damaged.

PREVENTING FAMILY FEUDS

Certainly neither the father nor the mother foresaw their remaining children being split down the middle and never communicating again – if they had, they would have altered their estate plan. The problem is, in terms of estate planning, we think about the financial and not the personal. We work hard at deciding who's going to inherit money and real estate, but not necessarily the personal items we own that could have real meaning to certain children or other relatives.

That's why I always urge my clients to create a legacy that won't fracture a family, but will, instead, bring it together and hopefully even strengthen it.

My eleven year-old son recently asked me, "What do you think happens if you die"? I told him that until science devises a way for us to live forever, it is not a matter of "if" but "when." Now, many parents would avoid having this kind of conversation with a child at all – but that's just the kind of thinking that leads to the tragic ending of the story just described.

Developing open communication and learning to be comfortable with the idea of death is the first step to effective estate planning. Once we liberate ourselves from the fear of discussing this taboo subject, we are open to the dialogue and can talk about what is truly meaningful in our lives. Making sure that we share these ideas over time will better prepare our loved ones in the event of our death, and pave the way for estate planning that encompasses our shared family values. At the most basic level, these conversations allow us to plan in a manner that can prevent objectionable surprises or unanticipated outcomes, which often degenerate quickly into divisive family squabbles.

Working with a *relationship-based estate planning attorney* can help you with this process of opening yourself up to these kinds of conversations and preparing a realistic estate plan that takes into account emotional factors as well as financial ones. A relationship-based estate-planning attorney is an attorney who is aware that your wealth extends beyond money. This attorney focuses on ensuring that your estate plan encompasses *all* aspects of who you are - not just your material wealth, but also your educational, spiritual, and philanthropic values, to name just a few.

Most people actually want these values to be reflected in their legacy; they're just not sure how to make that happen and most estate planning attorneys aren't much help. They think their job is limited to producing estate-planning documents focusing on money and tangible assets. That's it. No long-lasting relationship results between attorney and client. The client receives the documents and the lawyer sends them on their way, generally without a follow-up unless the client initiates it.

The relationship-based estate planning attorney's approach is very different. Not only are these professionals concerned with your deeper core values as well as your money and holdings, but they also emphasize and actively cultivate a lifelong relationship with the client; a relationship based on mutual understanding so that the lawyer can provide a lifetime of legal guidance and provide the best advice about the family, assets and the issues that may come up in the event of death.

Taking this kind of holistic approach to an estate is much healthier in the long run for any family. In some situations, it may be difficult for everyone involved to be completely satisfied with how an estate is handled – but at least they can have their say while the process is going on.

The key is *open communi*cation – and making sure that what will happen when the person passes away is discussed before that tragic event actually happens. It's better to try to address conflicts now, rather than when everyone is grieving and in a fog of emotion.

If you would like to work with a relationship-based estate planning attorney, one of the best places to look is the Family Wealth Planning Institute (which you can access at http:// personalfamilylawyer.com). You may also search for a Personal Family Lawyer in your neighborhood (Personal Family Lawyers are a nationwide group of attorneys committed to relationship and values-based estate planning).

The biggest source of hurt feelings and misunderstandings is a simple failure to communicate. A relationship-based estate planning attorney can help you break down the barriers to effective communication and keep your family united. And that's worth more than any size inheritance.

ABOUT CHRISTINE

Attorney Christine E. Faulkner's estate planning practice focuses on helping families enhance their lives today for a secure future tomorrow. Christine guides her clients in making the best legal and financial decisions during their lifetime to ensure the well-being of their families. Each plan is designed to meet the unique needs and goals of the cleint, while also preserving family traditions and beliefs. Her practice includes family protection, wealth preservation and family values-based planning, as well as planning for unmarried couples, and divorced individuals. No matter where you are in life, just starting out or enjoying a blissful retirement, married or single, Christine will help you create a plan to meet your goals for loved ones today and for years to come.

Christine graduated from New York Law School in 1990. From 1989-1990, Christine served as a law Clerk to the Honorable Justice Karla A. Moskowitz, on the Supreme Court of New York, drafting bench decisions and legal memoranda on pending Supreme Court cases. Christine worked for a large litigation firm in Southern California before becoming Corporate Counsel for Kemper Insurance Company.

In 2001, Christine E. Faulkner, Esq. became a Partner in the firm, Cava & Faulkner. Christine is a member of WealthCounsel, a collaborative nationwide network of estate planning attorneys, and the Advisors Forum, a nationwide organization comprised of estate-planning professionals, including attorneys, tax and financial planners who utilize cutting-edge techniques for sophisticated planning. Christine focuses her practice on Estate planning because this allows her the opportunity to help both individuals and families secure their futures for health and prosperity.

Christine has a passion for athletics and the outdoors. Christine swam competitively from the age of 7 until she was 22. During her athletic career, Christine was named an All-American Athlete when tying a National record. She was also inducted into the Sacramento Athletic Hall of Fame for outstanding performance and commitment.

Christine's biggest joy is spending time with her husband and business partner, David Cava, along with their two wonderful boys, Daniel and Cameron.

CHAPTER 13

'THAT WILL NEVER HAPPEN TO ME' – THE MYTH!

BY TERESA DE FORD, ESQ.

No matter how prepared you think you are to face death, all of that goes out the window when you hear the awful news that a friend or family member has died unexpectedly.

I've always thought of myself as a person who was not afraid of death. In the small mid-Michigan town that I grew up in I lived across the street from the sole funeral home in town. The elderly couple that ran the funeral home were like grandparents to me when I was young. I often stayed with them at their apartment in the back of the funeral home and never thought twice about running in to say "hi" even if there was a coffin in the viewing area.

Throughout my childhood and early adulthood, I had experienced the death of several family members - some expected and some not; some accidental and some intentional. Due to its proximity to the only funeral home in town, our house became the gathering place for family and friends to lean on each other and consume all the food that was lovingly brought by our friends and neighbors. At fifteen, a very close childhood friend died after a long and misunderstood illness. Throughout my high school years, too many kids from my community died in senseless car accidents, and I watched the cars line up for funeral after funeral right across the street. I was no stranger to death and loss, but nothing prepared me for the morning almost two years ago when I learned that the father of one of my eight year old son's best friends and a good friend of mine had died unexpectedly. As a parent, it finally hit me that regardless or whether you fear death, you should fear about what happens to those who are left behind.

That morning was like any other summer morning. I was dropping my oldest at summer camp and, as I got out of the car, another friend was arriving to drop off her kids. She looked stricken and said "Kelly's sister just called me. Ken died last night." We were both speechless. Ken hadn't been sick as far as we knew. Now there was talk of heart issues. Their family had just been to our house for dinner and swimming the week before. This couldn't be real. My reaction was visceral. I felt sick to my stomach – sick at thinking about what Kelly must be going through, sick at what their son was going through, sick at the thought of how I was going to tell my own 8 ½ year old and worried about how he would handle it.

My oldest son had gone to a local Montessori school from the time he was five months old until he graduated kindergarten there at 6 ½. He made wonderful lifelong friends at that school. Many of the parents bonded and became fast friends as well. After my son and his friends moved on from the Montessori school, they ended up at various different schools throughout the community. We tried to get together throughout the school year but with ever increasing busy schedules, that was often difficult. So we made a plan – so the kids could spend more time together, several of the moms got together and arranged for all the kids to go to the same summer day camp. This made us moms happy too. We got to see each other dropping off and picking up every night and have our girl time fix. We had a pact that when one of us was running late, the first parent to arrive at the day camp would sign out all the kids and wait for the other parents in the parking lot. Often we would all end up at a local restaurant to continue hanging out. We were a close knit group to say the least.

And now one of our close knit group was gone - in an instant. As I lay in bed that night, I couldn't stop thinking about what I would do if I was in Kelly's place. What would I do if my husband was suddenly gone? Although I inevitably thought about how I would make ends meet or handle two kids as a single parent if I were in that situation, what struck me the most was the worry about how I would help my boys. How would I help my boys through the pain and the heartbreak they would endure if they unexpectedly lost their father at such a young age? How would I help them remember and honor their father's legacy? I could barely breathe thinking about the pain that Kelly and her son were going through.

As we all got through the funeral, more and more "bits" of information came out. Ken had failed, or had perhaps felt he was unable, to obtain life insurance. He didn't have a will.

Ken had handled all the family finances and Kelly didn't even know the password to the computer where he kept all the files and information regarding the family's assets. Now, not only was Kelly dealing with the loss of her husband and her son's father, she was thrown into a legal and financial mess that she was going to need to sort out for them to be able to move on. Kelly of course turned to me for advice but, not being an estate planning lawyer at the time, I could only refer her to another lawyer – someone that I had no idea of knowing whether they would be the right lawyer for the job. I felt helpless and guilty that I wasn't able to be a better resource for her.

Part of me was mad at Ken. How could he have not had life insurance? How could he have not have had a will? How could he have left Kelly completely in the dark about their finances? And how could she have allowed him to keep her in the dark (although I am sure that he saw this as "protecting" her).

I could hardly be judgmental though. As a personal injury trial attorney, I handled fatality cases every day and knew the devastation that a person's death caused their family. Yet my oldest son was seven years old and I was pregnant with my youngest son before I ever even talked to a lawyer about having wills drawn up for me and my husband. I only did it then because another lawyer in my office kept bugging me about it.

Even after we had the will drawn up and guardian provisions in place, I delayed signing for months because I just wasn't sure if I had made the right decision about who should be the guardian for my children if something happened to both me and my husband. If something had happened to us in the meantime, all of our planning would have been for nothing. We were also woefully unprepared financially if something did happen. My husband didn't have any life insurance beyond the small policy that his employer purchased for him (assuming he remained employed there), and I had only a measly $100,000 policy in addition to the $50,000 policy my firm offered. My husband was the financially clueless one in our family; he was more than happy to let me handle all of that stuff and wash his hands of the details – never thinking about what he would do if I suddenly weren't there to take care of it.

Ken's death sparked something in me. From a spiritual perspective, I became much more conscious of trying to live in the present moment and letting go of what really didn't matter. I couldn't be in control of death but I could control how I lived. Just as importantly, I realized that I could control the legal and financial problems that can arise when someone dies. I wanted to make sure that what happened to Kelly didn't happen to anyone else that I knew, and I wanted to educate as many people as I could on how to make sure that it didn't happen to them. It was then that I started to focus my law practice on helping people protect their families.

If I had known then what I know now, I would have counseled Ken and Kelly to share information regarding their finances. Even if you are the spouse with primary responsibility for the finances, you act out of love when you empower your husband or wife with the information they would need to protect themselves and your family if you weren't here. If you are the spouse who normally stays out of the finances, for whatever reason, don't feel that you are showing distrust for your spouse if you ask to know what is going on with the family's finances and where all the documents and files are kept. By doing so, you show your love and concern for your family and your willingness to take on that role if you ever need to do so. Sit down today with your spouse and make a list of all your property, all your insurance policies, all your banking, brokerage and retirement accounts, and all the passwords necessary to access those accounts. Be sure to include the value of all the property and accounts and all identifying information such as account numbers and property descriptions. Sit down with a financial planner or insurance agent and evaluate your financial needs for now and in the future.

I also would have told Ken and Kelly that any will is better than no will. But the financial issues that arise when one or both spouses die pale in comparison to what can happen to the kids. At a minimum, Ken and Kelly should have nominated guardians for their son in case something happened to both of them. With Kelly now being a solo parent, naming guardians for her son is even more important. It doesn't matter whether you have $100 or $1 million, every parent must ensure that someone they trust is designated to take care of their children should something happen to them.

What many parents don't realize is that it is just as important to designate short term or temporary guardians for their children as it is to name permanent, long term guardians. First, if the persons you have named as long term guardians do not live close, someone will need to step in and care for your children immediately until the long term guardians can arrange to get there. Second, if you and/or your spouse are simply physically or mentally incapacitated, the long term guardian provisions in your will do not kick in. Designation of short term guardians that can step in quickly will protect your children in such a situation until you or your spouse are able to care for the children again.

And if you think, "Well, somebody in my circle of friends or family will take care of my children if something happens to me", …think again. They may not get the chance. If you do nothing to arrange for long term guardians for your children, a court will decide who should care for your children, and they may pick someone you would never pick. If you don't name short term guardians for your kids, CPS may become their guardian until everything can be sorted out. I know there is no parent that would want that for their children if they only knew what could happen.

We can come up with a million reasons why these terrible things will never happen to us or how things would be different if they did, but are you really willing to take that chance? For too many years I was that person, the one who didn't think it could happen to me and that everything would be okay. But every day we hear about accidents on the news where one or both parents is killed, leaving behind young children. Just today, a lawyer that I have been working with on a litigation matter called to ask if we could put the case on hold for a month while she took a leave of absence. Her 39 year old husband and law partner of ten years died unexpectedly last week, leaving her with two children under the age of 5. I hope and pray for her sake that she and her husband had talked about the inevitable event of one of their deaths and that in struggling with the emotions of losing her husband, business partner and the father of her children, she will not also have to go through the same financial struggles and probate problems that my friend Kelly went through.

ABOUT TERESA

Born on Christmas Eve 1966 in Lansing, Michigan, Teresa DeFord, Esq. grew up in the small, Mid-Michigan farming community of Ovid. Teresa later studied political philosophy and criminal justice at Michigan State University.

While at Michigan State, Teresa had the opportunity to participate in two internships with the U.S. Drug Enforcement Administration in Washington, D.C. Teresa's internships turned into a fascinating five year career with the DEA as an Intelligence Research Specialist, which took her from Washington, D.C. to San Francisco, California, and finally to Houston, Texas.

After five years with the DEA, Teresa started law school at the University of Houston Law Center. During law school, Teresa became a member of the Phi Delta Phi legal fraternity and was inducted into the Order of the Barons. Teresa was also the Senior Articles Editor for the Houston Law Review during her third year of law school. Teresa graduated from the University of Houston Law Center *cum laude* and was admitted to the Texas bar in 1995. She was admitted to the Louisiana bar in 2001.

Over the last 15 years, Teresa's legal practice has focused primarily on personal injury defense trial law, with an emphasis on trucking and oilfield injury litigation defense. Teresa has also handled business and employment law matters and numerous appeals. Recently, Teresa has found a passion in helping people learn how to best protect their families and businesses and she has expanded her practice to focus on that need.

Because of her passion for helping the people and businesses in her community, Teresa is very active in The Woodlands community. She is on the board of directors for both The Woodlands and Montgomery County Bar Associations, and The Community Clinic, a local free health clinic. Teresa also enjoys playing golf and is active with a women's golf organization called Women on Course. Teresa is also active in The Woodlands Chamber of Commerce and is a 2009 graduate of Leadership Montgomery County.

Teresa has been married to her husband Mark, a computer engineer she met while at Michigan State, since 1992. She and Mark have two busy boys (10 and 3) and the family resides in The Woodlands, Texas.

CHAPTER 14

LEGACY OF YOUR ACTIONS

BY R. DEDE SOTO, ESQ.

The legacy of your actions today will determine the legacy you leave behind for your loved ones.

Besides creating a loving home for our children, most parents want to leave a rich legacy of values and finances to enhance the lives of their children, especially young children. We all know this and yet very few of us put any conscious thought into it. It's always something you will take care of later or teach your children someday. Well, later never happens and suddenly one or both parents have passed and the children are left behind. The unexpected actually happens!

We spend so much time worrying about where our kids will go to school and what activities they'll be engaged in, but very rarely do we take the time to consider the values we are teaching them and the legacy we would leave behind –

should the unthinkable happen.

Instead, what happens is that our values are passed on by example or default. And sometimes those examples may not accurately reflect the messages we really would want to send or pass on if we actually stopped to think about it. What kind of examples are you teaching your children right now? Do you have your financial and legal house in order so that you may take full advantage of all financial resources available to you and your family – should something happen to you? Do you have guardians named for your children? What about guardians named until your permanent guardians can get to them? Have you documented your choices? Are there enough finances to provide for your loved ones? Have you captured your values, goals, dreams, and hope for you loved ones? What about addressing your fears and concerns for your loved ones so that you may have peace of mind?

It is a lot to take in and digest. If you are like most people, you are being stretched in so many directions that it is amazing to you that you even get through each day. You are just "too busy" to take the time to protect your loved ones. If you really want to protect your loved ones you must carve out the time now. When you set up an estate plan and meet with a personal family lawyer, you are ensuring that your assets will be passed on the way you want, and to whom you want.

The consequences of doing nothing, or your default plan, are represented in a story about Joe and Mary. Both 36 years young, actively engaging in all life has to offer with full days seven days a week. They are married with two boys ages seven and nine, and one girl who is five. Education is very important to both Joe and Mary and they have made sacrifices to start the kids in private school, since they were unable to. Joe, a successful entrepreneur works long hours to provide for his family. His wife Sue recently left a high paying corporate position to help Joe with his entrepreneurial businesses, and be able to spend more time with their children. Joe and Mary are very active in their community and lead a healthy Southern California lifestyle. Juggling the commitments that come along with having three children and being an entrepreneur did not leave much time for extra activities. Juggling time and activities are tough, they do not have any family nearby and have to depend on each other to get the kids to and from their activities. The closest relatives are Mary's sister and Joe's uncle and his wife. Mary's sister is only 30 and lives in Arizona, but has similar values and beliefs of Joe and Mary. Then there was Joe's uncle and his wife who live in Northern California, and who are estranged at the moment, and while they had two children of their own, they certainly do not approve of the things they are teaching their children.

Joe and Mary had discussed the fact that they needed to name guardians and meet with an attorney to establish an estate plan should something happen to them, but decided against it since they were only 36 and healthy. They felt that they didn't want to take the time or incur the expense that would be involved. They concluded it was not necessary at this time in their life and would take care of those matters when they were older. Besides they knew they wanted Mary's sister to be the guardian should something happen to the two of them. Life was too hectic and busy with three young children. Well, at 36, Joe died in his sleep, and thus the unexpected occurred.

The rest of this story only focuses on the financial aspects, and does not discuss the emotional mourning and shock that took place with Sue and her children.

Here is a summary of their accumulations: Most of their money was going into their entrepreneurial businesses, however they had accumulated a few assets. Their home appraised for $650,000, a rental property with Joe's friend, acquired prior to marriage, worth approximately $400,000, checking and savings accounts total $10,000, a 401(k) account, $200,000 in Sue's name and a SEP IRA $150,000 from Joe's businesses.

They had no life insurance, and of course, no estate plan in place. Banking accounts had a payable on death and the SEP IRA had a named beneficiary, Mary, so those accounts would not go through probate. However, probate would not be avoided on the rental property since it was held as tenants in common with Joe's friend.

The biggest asset Joe was missing was life insurance. There were not enough assets to take care of his wife and she knew very little about his businesses, as she only recently started assisting Joe. Thus, the value of the business was his time and effort, very income wealthy but no real plan in place to establish a sale price for the business. The assets they had acquired were certainly not sufficient to allow the kids to continue with their private school and fund their college education… And definitely not enough to allow Sue to continue to stay at home with the children.

Had Joe had either term or whole life insurance in place, the children and Sue would have benefitted financially, and it could have lessened the burden of finances as the family recovered from Joe's loss.

What happens next could easily have been avoided had the couple done some planning and protecting.

Due to the lack of finances, Mary is looking into selling their family home to lessen expenses until she is able to enter the work force again. The consequence of doing nothing is just what Mary is now experiencing.

Joe and Mary, like most married couples, held their personal residence as joint tenants with right of survivorship. They were told Joint Tenants would avoid probate, so they thought they held proper title. The good news is at the death of the first joint tenant, ownership automatically transfers to the survivor, instantly, as of the time of death. So yes, probate is avoided at the death of the first spouse. So while Mary takes full title to the house, it only prolongs probate. Upon Mary's death, the home will have to go through probate, even if it was Mary's intent to pass along the proceeds to the children.

The bad news, or tax consequences Mary will incur when she sells the home. Every inherited asset receives a "free step-up in basis." It is treated (for future income tax purposes) as costing the recipient its value on the date of death of the decedent. All pre-death capital gains are forgiven.

Joe and Mary bought their home for $400,000 as joint tenants. When Joe died, the home was valued at $650,000. Mary's tax cost (basis in the home: ½ of $400,0000 = $200,000) is $200,000. The survivor receives a step-up in basis only for the one-half 'inherited' through Joint Tenancy. Joe's share is valued at date of death value ($325,000), plus Mary's non-adjusted basis of $200,000 equals a total of $525,000. Subtracting this from the sale price of $650,000 gives her a taxable gain of $125,000 (plus capital gains) if she is forced to sell the family home.

A better choice for ownership for Joe and Mary would have been to hold title to the home as community property. At the death of one spouse, ownership easily transfers to the survivor (if no Probate claims are filed and there are no contrary provisions in the Will if one exists). Then at the death of the first spouse, both halves receive a "free step-up in basis." Why is this different from joint tenancy? It's just the law!

So, if Joe and Mary had bought the same house for $400,000 as community property, when Joe died and the value was worth $650,000, the survivor's tax cost basis is $650,000, (both shares are valued at the date of death value), and the above tax scenario would have been avoided.

The preferred choice for Joe and Mary would have been to hold title to the home in a Joint Trust as community property. Then at Mary's death, probate would have been avoided and the children would inherit the property.

The rental property Joe had with his friend Ted was held as tenants in common. While Joe held the rental property with Ted as tenants in common, it had never been transferred to joint ownership with Mary and thus was still his sole property. Again, the rental property will have to go through probate to decide who his one-half ownership will pass to. This will be a public process and will cost approximately 5% of his interest in the rental property, which at the time of his death was $400,000, so 5% of $200,000 is approximately $10,000 in probate fees alone. Once again, the preferred way to have held this would have been in the trust as either his sole property or community property with Mary. Then at his death, Mary would have owned the rental with Ted and avoided probate.

Now suppose Mary dies in a car accident a month later prior to selling the family home. The situation now becomes: three children left with no parents, no guardianship named, minimal finances and no trust in place. Joe and Mary's plan of doing nothing is now allowing probate to be their plan of action. So a judge will determine who the guardians will be – and here in California, probate could take up to 12 -18 months to sort through the estate. This is not to mention any other family members that may come forward, either claiming an interest in some of their assets or guardianship for the children (Joe's uncle and his wife). Mary's sister might not be the appointed guardian for the three children by the probate judge, since Joe's uncle is planning on coming forward and he looks better to the probate judge since he is married with children, and lives in California.

The 5% probate fees that will be paid is money that could have easily been avoided and would have allowed the children to continue to attend their private schools or even assisted with their college education.

Not only did Joe and Mary not leave sufficient finances, but their goals, wishes, values, and life experiences were left undocumented for the children. The children will never know why their parents were working so hard and never took the time to plan. While they were trying to provide a better life for their children, the stories will never be revealed to them in the way Joe and Mary would have wanted. So by not planning, the probate court is the default plan, and far more important, is the loss of the greatest asset of all - the intangibles. And guess what? They have learned by example, there was no plan in place.

To pass on a positive legacy of your actions would be to take measures now while you are young and healthy, no matter how young you are. You never know what tomorrow will bring. Why not ensure that your family and loved ones are taken care of if you are not able to raise them and pass on your values, goals, traditions and insights, and avoid the hassle and time consuming probate.

THE STEPS TO TAKE TO AVOID THE LEGACY THAT JOE AND MARY LEFT BEHIND.

STEP ONE:
NAME GUARDIANS

The first action step is to legally document the guardians for all three children. Establish both temporary and permanent guardians. When Mary was in her accident the kids were all in child care. While the childcare center had emergency phone numbers, they could not release the children to the emergency contacts because there were no legal documents in place giving anyone custodial authority. Had there been documents, the temporary legal guardians could have stepped in and taken the children. So yes, child protective services had to be called until someone could be located. The children were already about to experience the loss of their parents, and were now to be put into a stranger's custody? Even if Mary's sister who lives out of state had been named, she could not get to the children for a few days. So a temporary guardian would have been needed in this situation. And finally, we know that Joe's uncle will be attempting to gain custody of the children. Had guardianships been legally documented, this would have been avoided and out of the court's hands.

STEP TWO:
ESTABLISH A REVOCABLE LIVING TRUST

In order to leave a legacy that reflects your desires and values, you will need to establish a Revocable Living Trust (RLT). This is the first step to take to avoid probate, save on taxes, and protect the estate from predators. One of the most important aspects of establishing your Revocable Living Trust is transferring your assets into the Trust. This is called "funding." A trust does not avoid probate if it is not properly funded. The fundamental concept of using a trust to protect your loved ones is that all the rules and issues for the management and transfer of your property are included within the terms of the trust document. And what that means to you is that no court action is required to implement your wishes and you will be passing on a legacy of congruency for handling your finances when you are not able to do so. Some of the advantages of properly establishing a trust are:

1. Avoidance of probate.
2. Minimizing the delays and hassles of managing and transferring assets in a death probate action.
3. Costs of administering your trust assets are far less than the costs of going through probate.
4. Compared to property held in joint title, you can control how ownership of your property will pass even after your death through your trust.
5. Revocable Living Trust's (RLT's) are private and confidential. Survivors do not have to reveal the extent of the trust's assets through a public filing that would occur through the probate process.
6. Directing how and when your minor children will gain access to the finances you leave in place, without a probate judge giving your 18 year olds all the finances that you left them.
7. RLT's may protect assets for your loved ones through legacy planning. Legacy planning can provide for children who are not good with money and protects their inheritance from future divorces, judgments, bankruptcy, creditors and predators. (Seek professional assistance here).

STEP THREE:
TRANSFERRING YOUR ASSETS – FUNDING YOUR TRUST

So how do you fund your trust? Pending on the asset involved there are various ways to transfer your assets. Changing title on accounts and changing beneficiaries may sound like something easy to do, however there could be major tax effects of changing these assets without consulting an expert.

1. Most people's major asset is their home. All real estate is transferred by a transfer deed (or other appropriate method of transferring your real estate), in which the trustees (you decide who these are) of the trust are the owners of the home. Finally, you may need to obtain an endorsement to your title insurance to make sure adequate coverage is continued after the transfer.
2. Personal property is transferred by a bill of sale or other assignment document to your trustee.
3. Stocks and bonds held in your name are transferred to your trust by reissuing the certificate in the name of your trustee.
4. Investment accounts and bank accounts are transferred to your trust by having your financial advisor or banker change ownership on the accounts to your trustee.
5. IRAs, retirement plans, annuities, and life insurance generally will not have ownership transferred to your trust due to potential tax implications and must be evaluated on a case-by–case basis with the advice of qualified counsel.
6. Ownership and interest in private companies, partnerships and limited liability companies may

require an assignment or stock power and reissuing ownership certificates in the name of the trustee.

7. Inheritances, gifts, or lawsuit judgments not yet received, can generally be transferred by assignment to your trustee. (Again, professional consultation may be necessary.)

STEP FOUR:
HAVING SUFFICIENT FUNDS IN PLACE

Mary and Joe did not have sufficient funds to continue the lifestyle that Joe and Mary had wanted to provide for their family. After evaluating all your assets, you should also take into consideration the amount and type of life insurance. Whether it is term or whole, you should have sufficient funds to ensure that your loved ones are taken care of if you are unable to provide for them. And of course, you want to make sure these funds are being sufficiently managed by someone who is financially savvy.

Yes, had Joe and Mary taken the time to plan, this could have been avoided. The consequences of the prolonged process of probate, the dispute over guardianship and the cost involved would have ensured an easier transition, not to mention the extra finances that would have been provided. But what about all those intangibles we discussed earlier?

FINAL STEP:
PASSING ON THE INTANGIBLES

Joe and Mary were not able to pass on their values, wishes and dreams to their children. Their children were not old enough to hear many of the words that were said. At five, seven and nine years old, not all the messages were passed to them. What they will likely grow up knowing is that nothing was done to provide for them or leave a legacy that could be passed on to their children. They will never hear their parents' voices again. How can you avoid this?

The intangible legacy is one treasure that most children would cherish the most. You can capture what is most important to you. Whether it is about using money wisely, choosing a mate, or even a career? You can pass along secrets for a happy and successful life or give some advice based on your own personal experience that you would like your children to know. For example, you might depend on someone else for financial support, and thus value independence and want more than anything for your children (especially girls), to be independent.

The best way to document your stories is through an interview which is recorded – one that captures those values, insights and personal experiences that we have been talking about. So that years from now, your children will be able to hear your voice again and understand what you were all about.

Take the time now to pass on your treasures to those you love and adore.

ABOUT DEDE

R. DeDe Soto, Esq. established Soto Law Group so she could dedicate herself to the needs of growing families and business owners. DeDe has a broad background of legal experience.

Early in her legal career, she started practicing in family law and business litigation, and later on, she developed extensive real estate expertise. This expertise includes community planning/land-use entitlement, extensive negotiations with municipalities, local government and business owners on behalf of large real estate developers. Other areas of her expertise include environmental compliance, conservation easements, and complicated acquisition issues.

R. DeDe Soto, Esq. started her estate planning practice only on a referral basis several years ago, and recently made the transition to full-time with the Soto Law Group. To provide invaluable services for families and small business owners, she has continued her education at Chapman College School of Law (with LLM courses) and financial planning courses at University of California, Irvine (Financial Planning Certificate with only 1 more class). Incorporating her business knowledge and real estate expertise with her passion for coaching and teaching, she brings an invaluable combination to her estate planning clients.

Joining the Personal Family Lawyer® program was a natural fit for her. She had always believed that traditional estate planning, which implies, and often focuses only on, financial wealth and taxation was too limited and short-sighted. DeDe believes it's not only about passing on financial wealth, but also intellectual, spiritual and human wealth. As part of the Family Wealth Institution, she can provide a framework for a more holistic approach to family wealth planning. "We can actually pass on the clients' stories, insights and wisdom to their children, grandchildren and other loved ones so that they don't get lost when the clients pass away," she explains. She also appreciates that, through the Kids Protection Plan, her clients can rest assured, knowing that if something unexpected or unthinkable happens to mom and dad, the kids won't have to spend time in Child Protective Services/foster care until their permanent guardians can arrive on the scene. Additionally, she can protect the children's inheritance from later creditors and predators.

On a personal note, she is happily married to husband Robert, and they have a Chihuahua named Noodle. Both she and her husband are dedicated to assisting and protecting families.

Her undergraduate degree is from California State University of Fullerton, with a major in Psychology. She obtained her Juris Doctor degree from Western State University School of Law. Visit her website at: www. thesotolawgroup.com

CHAPTER 15

ARRANGE TO TRANSFER YOUR ASSETS FOR YOUR HEIRS SAKE

BY ROWEL MANASAN, ESQ.

When she heard the news that her sister and brother-in-law died in a tragic car accident, tears welled up in Veronica's eyes. This couldn't be true. Memories of them flooded her mind and the suddenness of their deaths filled her with grief. After she collected herself, Veronica knew, as one of the only close relatives residing in the United States, that she would be responsible for providing Robert and Rita Yano with a dignified funeral. She knew of no one else who would shoulder the responsibility. Her mother was wheelchair-bound and no other siblings would be able to manage putting together the funeral.

What lay before her however would be no easy task. Robert and Rita Yano were well known in the Rowland Heights community. They were heavily involved in St. Elizabeth Ann Seton, a church heavily populated by Filipinos. Filipino funerals tend to be very large affairs. Even folks who knew very little about Robert and Rita Yano would attend a funeral celebration on their behalf. The tragic killing of two well known Filipinos in the community would certainly bring a whole host of Filipinos to the funeral. Veronica's task was daunting.

Veronica was overwhelmed. She was retired and taking care of her ill, bedridden mother. Veronica lacked the money to put on the funeral celebration, so she asked her son as well as several other relatives if she could borrow the money to pay for the funeral. She convinced her son that he would be paid back through the money Robert and Rita left behind. Veronica believed that transferring wealth from one family to the next after death would be easy. In the Philippines, close relatives can easily access a dead sibling's money when they pass away. All Veronica needed to do in the Philippines would be to show proof that her sibling died and that she was a close relative.

However, in California, the transfer of wealth is not that simple. If you own real property, such as a house, or your assets are valued over $100,000, California law requires you to go through the Probate process if you die without a will. Unfortunately for Veronica, Robert and Rita Yano failed to draft a will or an estate plan. Soon enough, Veronica found herself in court trying to get the funeral expenses paid and handle Robert and Rita's property.

At the hearing, Veronica discovered that she had no power to handle Robert and Rita's property. Robert Yano's distant niece, Desiree Sales, applied to be the personal administrator of Robert and Rita's property or "estate." The personal administrator is the person appointed to handle all the property of the deceased. The attorney for Desiree Sales argued that all Rita's property belonged to Robert's estate and thus only relatives of Robert Yano had the power to control all the Yano property. Because Rita died instantly in the car crash, and Robert died several hours later in the hospital, that attorney argued Rita's property transferred from her estate to Robert Yano's estate. Since Rita did not have a will, according to California default rules of "intestate law"; Robert would be the next heir to receive Rita's estate. Since Desiree Sales appeared to be the only living relative who would handle the estate, the court named Desiree Sales as the administrator of the estate.

Veronica was at a loss. People still advised her to apply to become administrator of the estate, but since Veronica had very little money and did not want to pay for the cost of hiring a probate attorney, Veronica did not petition the court to be named an administrator. Indeed, the attorney for Desiree Sales made it clear that none of the money belonged to Rita Yano's family.

Unfortunately, Veronica had very little to cover the funeral expenses. Immediately, Veronica approached Desiree about how these costs would be covered. Desiree agreed to allow Veronica to take money out of the Yano bank account to pay for the costs. Buoyed by Desiree's ok, Veronica, with death certificate in hand, marched into the bank and took out approximately $30,000.00. In the Philippines, it's often the case that when a family member dies, the next of kin provide proof of the death and they can receive the money from the accounts. In the United States, only the personal representative may be allowed to take any money from the bank accounts and any other person must receive court permission in order to handle the money. Nevertheless, Veronica managed to take this money out of the bank account. Veronica felt relieved that she could now pay for the funeral.

Hundreds attended the service at Queen of Heaven Cemetery. The community, brought together by the suddenness and tragic nature of their deaths, attended the funeral and the reception that followed. Thousands of dollars were spent, but Veronica felt it was her duty to provide such a celebration.

In addition, Veronica also felt obligated to pay off debts that her sister and brother-in-law incurred throughout their lifetime. A few debtors came to Veronica and asked that some of that money be paid to them. Unwittingly, she agreed to the arrangement believing that it was the right thing to do. However, all of these actions were extremely illegal.

While Veronica was paying off all these debts, she, unfortunately, was breaking the law. Veronica had no authority to take this money from the Yanos bank accounts. To make matters worse, Desiree Sales, the person who sanctioned Veronica's taking of the money for funeral expenses, had run off with $17,000.00 and was nowhere to be found. Desiree Sales' attorney, Walter Scott, believed that Desiree and Veronica were conspiring to steal all the money in the estate. Both Desiree and Veronica were the two people who had access to all the accounts. When Veronica explained that Desiree had sanctioned her taking money from the account, the large exorbitant funeral fee, and the payments made to creditors, Walter Scott did not believe a word. And why would he? Desiree ran off with the money, and the funeral expenses claimed by Veronica were unusually high. The attorney pointed out that Veronica had absolutely no authority to pay off the creditors in the estate without court approval, and that none of these transactions could possibly be bona fide transactions. With little left in the estate, Scott went after Veronica and Desiree in Probate court, claiming that Desiree embezzled funds while Veronica flat out stole from the Yanos.

In court, Veronica had a very difficult time explaining her side of the case. She had very little money for an attorney, and didn't bother contacting one because she knew she couldn't afford it. As she stood in front of the Judge, Veronica explained in broken English that she did nothing wrong and that she did not steal the money. She did not understand how paying for funeral expenses and the Yanos' debts could be construed as a terrible thing in court. Her command of English also made it difficult for her to express her position as well as understand the court's request for an accounting of the costs. In subsequent hearings, Veronica stated that she did not have the money, and she likewise failed to produce the receipts in a timely fashion – despite having them in her possession.

Due to Veronica's inability to provide the necessary documents to the Judge, and with Walter Scott's insistence that Veronica and Desiree conspired to steal the money, the Judge ordered Veronica to pay back the full amount of the money to the court, or face potential criminal charges. Veronica was forced to hire an attorney.

During the attorney's investigation, the attorney pointed out that Veronica was in fact entitled to be the personal representative of Rita Yano's estate. Probate Code Section 6403 and 103 essentially states when a wife and husband die within a 120 hour time period without a will or living trust, the husband and wife's property would be split in half, with one half of the property going to the wife's heirs and one half of the property belonging to the husband's heirs. Had Veronica hired an attorney at the beginning of the probate proceedings, she would have been entitled to administer the estate of Rita Yano. Instead, Veronica's attempts at saving money backfired. Not only was Veronica forced to payback all the funeral money to the court, but the court also threatened her with imprisonment if she failed to produce the money. Veronica was forced to wait until the end of the probate proceedings, which took several more months.

Despite the best of intentions, Veronica had to endure the vitriol of an angry Probate lawyer, potential prison time, and thousands of dollars. Had Robert and Rita Yano put together an estate plan through the use of a fully funded living trust, they could have avoided having a distant niece embezzle $17,000.00 out of their estate and completely disappear, and the only next of kin who was willing to provide them with a proper funeral would not have had to face criminal charges, or wait for several years before being reimbursed for those costs. Also, had they worked with the right kind of attorney, Veronica would have had someone to turn to – to help her administer the estate on their passing.

Their failure to plan not only cost their family thousands of dollars in attorneys fees, court costs, and appraisal fees, but it nearly cost Veronica her freedom as well as her peace of mind. At times, she wept in court and spent many sleepless nights dealing with the situation.

The only foolproof way to avoid afflicting your family members with the scenario faced by Veronica is through a fully funded living trust. A living trust allows a person to avoid probate by transferring everything the deceased person owns into a living trust. The beauty of a living trust is that as the creator of a living trust, you still have all the traits of owner-ship. You can buy, sell, and use your property any way you want while you and your spouse are alive. You even have the power to revoke the trust if you don't want to place all your property within the trust. When you pass away, you have the power to name who will manage all your property and who will receive it. Also, you control when your family members receive their inheritance. You can even provide instructions in your trust which would set aside money specifically for your funeral expenses. And finally, your family members will not have to deal with outsiders who will attempt to take control of your property and/or embezzle the money. By avoiding the court process through a fully funded living trust, the transition will be a hundred times easier for your family members.

A fully funded living trust is the 'surefire' way to help your family members avoid a costly and oftentimes complicated probate process.

ABOUT ROWEL

Rowel Manasan has dedicated his life and business to helping young families in the community grow through education and cultural awareness. He is a frequently requested guest on The Filipino Channel, where he speaks on subjects ranging from Dual Citizenship to Civil Rights and Estate Planning. Unlike other lawyers, Rowel focuses his law practice on the relationship he develops with his clients and not just the documents he provides, which means you know you are going to have someone to turn to in times of challenge.

As a schoolteacher at Covina High School, Rowel witnessed firsthand how children within the foster care system suffered greatly – both personally and academically. That's why his mission is to educate and provide parents with the tools necessary to ensure their children are always taken care of by the people you choose, in the way you want. Rowel hosts educational events ranging from the 9 Steps to Ensuring Your Kids are raised the Way You Want by the People You Want, to his popular Guardianship Nomination Workshop, and to Asset Protection for young families. For more information on how you can ensure the well-being of your children, grandchildren and future generations through the power of legal planning, and a relationship with a Personal Family Lawyer®, contact Rowel Manasan at (909) 843-6427 or email him at rowel@manasanlaw.com.

CHAPTER 16

WISDOM IS THE LEGACY

BY MARTHA J. HARTNEY, ESQ.

I t was a small pile. No more than nine inches around; the remnants of my father's life. We stood in a semi-circle around the bed, the familiar floral pattern of my parent's 20-year-old polyester bedspread cupping his only worldly possessions. That was all that was left of him, a man who had loomed large in my little girl's memory. He was so big to me, even laying in his casket earlier that morning ... cold, rock-like hands dwarfing mine. He was so large partly because I was so small, partly because dads cast very long shadows.

My husband broke the silence, "Is that all he had? I've got garages full of crap. Hah!" My sisters glared. There were six or seven medals; a money clip; a few cuff links, a couple letters, one I recognized from me; some old foreign coins and bills; and one glimmering solid gold Rolex.

That was it. All that was left of a 78-year old man.

You'd think he died poor. But he didn't. My father was a great man, he died with the riches of friendships lasting his lifetime, experiences he couldn't have imagined as a boy, and a lot of family.

But as I stood there wishing I could pick up that little pile and hold each and every piece tight to my chest, I understood how little I knew of my father. What I knew, what I know could fill a single page.

As a girl, I yearned for him to tell me about himself, to describe his work to me, to tell me about his childhood, his early fatherhood, his flying adventures, his tragedies, and his lessons. When I was born, my father was already 46 years old and his face had always had lines etched into them. His hair was always thin and speckled with gray, teeth slightly yellowed. I'd never known my father as a young man with a full head of hair and smooth handsome face.

That's because I am the youngest of ten children. His past was far, far away from the everyday demands of raising a family of ten. I was the child of his age and I knew nothing of his youth.

My roots in the world have often felt a little thin and shallow. My seven sisters and two brothers seemed so strong and vibrant, like their roots dug deep down into the earth of my parents' lives. They were familiar with stories of our family's origin in Ireland, my parents' romance, their tales of drama and adventure during the war and after. I never quite got the hang of their language. They shared associations, jokes, and memories that I just didn't get. So when I looked at my dad and mom, I wished I knew about more about them. I wanted my history. I yearned for heritage.

By the time I got to college, I started asking my father to write his stories down, sometimes even begging. He shook his head saying he had no talent for writing, which I knew wasn't true since he'd written letters to me from time to time. He had a skill with words he never admitted. Eventually, his excuse for not putting his past down on paper became—"I don't like the word 'I' and if I write about my life, it'll be a bunch of I's all over the page and nobody wants to read that."

And all I wanted was the I's.

Later, I asked to interview him and record his stories. He grudgingly agreed. But then I had a baby and was too busy trying to be a good mom. I never got to record him. He died when my son was a toddler.

When I was in high school, I had a few years with just my mother, father and me. With one left in the nest, life was pretty good. We got along very well, the three of us.

But the missing piece for me was that father thing, that missing dad. He was a pilot and was gone a lot. And when he was home, he was distant emotionally. He was exhausted from raising kids for 45 years. There was no gas left in his tank for the rigors of another daughter.

I got involved in a youth group when I was 14. I'd started to take my spiritual life seriously, maybe too seriously. The youth group was lead by a younger redheaded couple, Mike and Marilyn. They had six redheaded kids whose names all began with "M." I loved them. I loved them with all my heart because they knew each other. They spent time together. They worked through their problems. They shared stories and history and love together, and with all of the teenagers they were surrounded by. They taught us how to be a family for each other, even when our own families weren't all that present.

My mother finally had the time for self-reflection. She 'got religion' at about that time and started studying Catholicism. Each morning, she woke early and sat in her leopard print robe drinking coffee in the living room. She read the bible from cover to cover. And then did it again. She transcribed her favorite bible and inspirational passages in a journal each morning and before long, had amassed a pile of journals. Over the years, my usual gift to her was a new journal. She shared her favorites now and then and did her best to connect with me, to walk with me spiritually.

My mother believed for years that I was supposed to be a nun. She didn't really give that up until I got married. And even then, she held out hope that I would one day take holy orders. But that was not to be. I never did tell her that I'd left the church; that God and I had had a talk about religion and decided that a better path for me would be a broader approach. Still, I loved that she had begun to dig into her deeper meaning during those years when I was at home alone with them.

I asked her to promise me only one thing out of all her possessions when she passed. I wanted her journals. Not just one or two divided between my sisters and myself, but every one of them. I didn't feel greedy for her jewelry, her silver, her formal dinnerware, or her mink. I wanted the words that meant most to her, set down by her own hand. And I wanted them all to myself. She promised that they would be mine because, she said, no one else wanted them.

After my father died, Mom moved in with my sister Mary in Virginia. And later moved to Oregon to live Anne. She visited Janis and me in California a few times a year. But on one occasion, she didn't go back. She got sick. She stayed. She moved into an assisted living apartment. Her place was very small compared to the large houses they used to have to accommodate their family. But she'd had it painted a butter yellow that kept her cheery and upbeat. She rarely complained of being lonely, but you could tell in her voice that she was.

My husband and I moved to Colorado. I visited every few months until she got sick again. Then it became every few weeks. She spent four months in the hospital on a constant flow of oxygen. On one visit, I stayed at her apartment and noticed that the journals were not there. When I asked, she said she'd long since thrown them away. They were just her favorite passages and no one else would want them. I was devastated. She had not thought I was serious about wanting them and had pitched them in one of her moves.

My mom grew tired of being tethered to oxygen and coughing incessantly. Her sides ached, her stomach was never quite right. She wanted to go home to my father. She picked a date to die.

Nine of us came, and her sister, a son-in-law, a daughter-in-law, and several of her grandchildren. We spent the last four or five days and nights in round-the-clock Mom-watch. We talked. She made time alone with each of us to give us her final words of wisdom and her apologies.

She beat us all in Scrabble.

She put her hands on our faces and cried.

She gave me her blessing to divorce my husband.

On a Friday morning, we all followed her into the ICU and surrounded her bed. The doctors gave her morphine and other drugs to keep her from feeling anxious. As she was drifting off, she said to us in a half-stern voice, "Now no joking around y'all. This is serious business. I don't want you all laughing while I'm dyin'.' "

My sister asked if she'd like to tell us anything else, "Yeah," she said glancing at her dentures on the side table. "Hang on to your teeth. The final words of an 83-year old dimwit,"

She settled into a sleep that wasn't quite real. The doctor took off her oxygen and we sat waiting in silence for a long time until my aunt hummed, then sang, "And I will raise you up, on eagle's wings…." My mother's breathing became labored. Her indrawn breath took a lot of effort. Her lips became lax and her exhale made her lips blubber like a raspberry.

Anne piped in, "Oh, pppppfffffffttttt, yourself!"

We couldn't help it. After the howling died down, the stories started to flow, stories about Mom's better and worse moments. Her disastrous tomato aspic, the many dresses she made for each of her daughters, the first time she was overheard swearing. The way she danced with our father.

The day before she died, she told us that her life had been a grand adventure, bigger than she ever imagined it could be. She'd traveled the world, seen the Depression, the wars, rapid industrialization, advances in technology that boggled her mind. She was even able to video chat the one daughter who could not make it to her bedside. She had raised ten kids and had not lost one. She'd seen us through most of the major thresholds of our lives. She had seen her last grandchild be brought into the world, my second son, and several great grandchildren too.

She was giddy to have had so much of everything in it; joy, sorrow, pain, suffering, laughter, adventure, change, and more change. There was nothing left for her to do but to go back to the love of her life, our dad, who she loved beyond words despite the horrible moments they'd had.

When she gave me her blessing to start my life over, I had asked her why she'd stayed with my father when times were really tough. She said, "I had nowhere to go Martha. It was a different time and we had something very special. We enjoyed each other."

"Mom, I don't have that with my husband. And I have somewhere to go. I'm going to law school," I said.

"That's the Martha I remember. I didn't like the way you changed when he started making a lot of money. Dad knew he wasn't going to treat you well."

"Well, why didn't he say so?"

"He did in his own way. You just don't remember."

Over the years, my mom had shared her stories, enough for me to have an idea of what her life was about. The gift she gave to me was her courage, her sense of gratitude, her fortitude in the face of overwhelming circumstances. I'd wanted those journals to remind me each day of my life of those things that helped her live hers.

My mother gave me one material thing, a lovely necklace that I never wear. I don't need it. It sits in a safe, waiting for me to give it to someone else. I realize that I have the one thing I wanted from her. Roots.

ABOUT MARTHA

Hartney Family & Estate Law is an estate planning practice serving all kinds of Colorado families. A later-in-life attorney, Martha Hartney opened the practice in 2010 to serve the people she loves because she is committed to helping moms and dads bring their greatest gifts into parenting fearlessly and with joy and making sure children are completely cared for if something happens to their parents.

Martha graduated from the University of Denver while being a full time mother of two sons. She focused her studies on family, juvenile, and estate law and served in the Boulder County District Attorney's Office; Larimer County Domestic Courts; and the Rocky Mountain Children's Law Center. Martha has served as a pro bono guardian ad litem representing abused and delinquent children. After law school, she was certified as a Child & Family Investigator through the Colorado Bar Association. She has also supported new mothers as a La Leche League Leader and been an advocate of attachment parenting and natural parenting.

CHAPTER 17

LEAVE A LEGACY FOR YOUR FAMILY

BY GARY L. WINTER, ESQ.

J ust what you wanted – another boring story from an estate planning attorney, right? I promise it's not! How many estate planning attorneys do you know that fly jets? Probably none. Believe it or not, in my previous career, I was a commercial airline pilot for a major U.S. carrier. I'm sure you are thinking… "Why would you leave such a great career to do estate planning?" Great question. Actually, it has something to do with leaving a legacy for *my own* family. Read on and I'll tell you my story and why it might impact your life in a powerful way.

MY STORY:
FROM FLIGHT PLANS TO ESTATE PLANS.

My family was a typical Air Force family, always moving around and traveling, taking tours of air bases and attending air shows. I loved the airplanes and wanted to fly since my earliest memories. My father was eventually stationed in the Washington D.C. area as he was promoted. We lived in the area for several years. While we were there, my mother was diagnosed with melanoma skin cancer, an aggressive and deadly variety. At first, she wasn't seriously impacted but over a two or three year period, the cancer spread and she began to struggle with other health issues.

My parents are from California, so after her illness became more severe, they made the decision to return there to be closer to family. After a three-year battle, my mother passed away at the young age of 46. I was the oldest, and I was only 19.

My parents prepared and planned for the tragedy the way they were advised to. They had life insurance, a burial plot, and some other things that dealt with the practical details of our lives. I'm sure the life insurance helped out, but frankly, I know it didn't leave the legacy that my mother really cared about.

You see, my mother was primarily concerned with what she was going to miss in my life and in the life of my younger brother. I know this from conversations I had with her in the weeks before she died. She wanted some way to share her wisdom, her values, her family history, and her spiritual heritage, because she knew she wasn't going to be able to be there for those pivotal life events in the future. For my mother, this was especially heart-wrenching, because her father died in a tragic accident when she was only four.

Knowing from personal experience how much my brother and I would miss her presence in the future, my mother even went so far as to attempt to make audio recordings in the hospital in the weeks before she died. Her thought was that these could be saved and heard at special life events such as graduations, weddings, first child, etc. But, she couldn't get through it physically and emotionally – she had waited too long. Her body was so weak and the emotions were too painful. She could not make the tapes.

Many years later now, my wife and three children miss the opportunity to know who my mother was. They miss her wise words, her family history, her spiritual heritage, her story, her *"legacy"*. The technology was there to record her own thoughts and her own words, but now they have to rely on those of us who remain, to remember and share our own interpretation. I don't even recall if my mother had a will! But I would give anything just to have those tapes so I could vividly be reminded of her legacy and share it with my kids.

I often wondered – why did she wait to share her legacy? My parents knew she was seriously ill for several years. They met with planners and they organized her affairs. But they planned for the transfer of her 'stuff', not her legacy. After a career change from pilot to attorney, I began helping families with their business and estate planning needs. I prepare wills, trusts, advance health care directives, powers of attorney and the like. One day, it occurred to me that nearly all the planning work I did, important as it was, was oriented toward 'stuff'. Law school, firms I worked with, practice guides were all oriented toward answering the practical questions: how we're going to pass title to this property or that account or who is going to be named trustee or guardian of the kids, who gets the car and who gets the vacation home. 'Stuff'. Just like the planners that advised my family, I was focused on the practical and ignoring the critical. I was planning for how my clients could leave their 'stuff' and ignoring how they could leave a legacy because that's how the entire financial and legal industry has always done it.

I know how important leaving a legacy was to my mother because she had grown up without a father. She knew what my brother and I would go through growing up without her. With only a little effort, so much more could have been done to leave a legacy for generations to come. I resolved that, for myself and for my mother, I will not ignore the important just to handle the practical. So, I resolved to offer an opportunity in my practice where clients can share their legacies with their current family and even future generations using digital recording technology. That information can even be virtually stored, so that it is protected from physical destruction. We are implementing these exciting tools as part of a more holistic, legacy-oriented approach to estate planning.

Are your grandchildren, great-grandchildren and great-great grandchildren important to you? Do you have a valuable legacy to share with them? If you haven't shared it already, why are you procrastinating? Read on for an easy-to-implement, three-step approach to communicating your legacy now.

THREE WAYPOINTS TO LEAVE YOUR LEGACY

A "waypoint" is an aviation term for a specific location. From your departure airport, your flight plan will consist of several, even dozens of waypoints to get you safely to your destination. If you're like most people, you're presently doing little or nothing to leave a legacy for your family. You may have downloaded some form documents from an internet website, used a paralegal to prepare some forms, or even consulted an attorney to take care of your stuff. But you're still not leaving a legacy and you know how critical it is. How do we get to the destination of leaving a legacy? Easy. Just follow my three Waypoints below.

WAYPOINT #I
ACT NOW: PROCRASTINATION IS THE ENEMY OF LEAVING A LEGACY.

The number one reason why I believe my mother did not leave us her legacy is because she waited too long. All those years of gradually becoming more ill and she didn't sit down alone for a couple of hours with a tape recorder to share her legacy. By the time she was ready, it was too late. She was too physically ill and it was just too emotionally painful to accomplish the task.

I've talked with many of my clients about this and they all say the same thing. They don't know what to say, they don't know if they can get through it without emotionally breaking down. Take it from me, waiting around until you feel ready sets you up to fail. It's a certainty that you will pass on. It is not a certainty that you will grow old prior to passing on. My mother wasn't particularly old when she died. She was only 46.

If you think you are paralyzed with fear of dealing with the issue of your own mortality now, imagine how difficult it will be in a crisis! I'm going to be honest with you - emotional crisis situations *will* prevent you from ever moving forward. So, if you don't act now, when things are as normal as they can be, you never will.

Act now, do not wait, do not make the mistake of thinking you have plenty of time to do this.

WAYPOINT #2
EXPAND YOUR PLANNING HORIZONS SO THAT THEY ARE *MORE THAN MONEY.*

The second reason why I believe my mother wasn't able to leave her legacy is because her advisors didn't facilitate it.

They didn't facilitate it because they were focused on life insurance and a will and a do-not-resuscitate order. All worthy things, but why does estate planning have to be limited to who gets what? Why not include your life story, the story of your family, your work, your values, your spiritual heritage, your skills and knowledge. These are the things that are truly valuable in life. Money can be made and spent, but a legacy will be lost in a generation or two unless someone is making an effort to share it with the next generation.

Another reason many advisors don't facilitate leaving a legacy is because they are not comfortable with it. They are just as uncomfortable with emotional matters as you are. I encourage you to seek an advisor that doesn't discount your feelings and the importance of the intangible things. Work with someone who believes in legacy transfer and incorporates tools to do that in their practice. It should be someone who will listen to you, validate you, and draw out the important details from you in a natural conversation. You can't get that from the internet downloads, the document prep services, or even most law firms.

Work with an advisor that believes in and will make it easy for you to leave a legacy.

WAYPOINT #3
BE SPECIFIC.

My mother tried to be specific. Her plan was to create an audio tape for my brother and me to listen to on specific, special occasions so that she could express her love and wisdom for us that way. The more specific you can be and the more detail you can provide to your family about your legacy, the more you will impact them for generations to come. Don't just sit down and write a letter. While the letter is not a bad thing, it's inevitable that you will not be able to cover all the areas and all of the subjects that your family will be interested in.

I suggest using audio or video recordings of you while you are speaking. This can be done in a natural, conversational format where your advisor is asking you to share some of your stories. An outline of important subjects and specific questions should be used to keep the conversation moving so that each important topic is covered.

Why do you need an advisor for that? I'll tell you. Because you'll never do it otherwise and you won't open up about the same things if it's your family asking you the questions. An objective third party that doesn't have the same emotional response to your legacy is an important piece of the equation. Don't try and do this alone.

Work with an advisor who has a plan.

FOLLOW THE WAYPOINTS TO LEAVING A LEGACY.

Now, don't just sit there smugly and think about what a nice idea this all would be. Do it! Remember, procrastination is the enemy of leaving a legacy. It happened in my family, and it's the number one reason my clients haven't done their own legacy planning. Follow the Waypoints to create a powerful, impacting legacy today.

Waypoint #1: Act Now.

It really doesn't have to be so bad! If you use an advisor who listens, validates and facilitates the process, it really isn't so scary. I meet with several clients each month to discuss serious financial and practical issues related to their incapacity and death. Sometimes people struggle a bit, but that's normal. If we can discuss financial things, why can't we discuss leaving a legacy?

Waypoint #2: Expand your planning horizons so that they are More Than Money.

Share your life story, the story of your family, your work, your values, your spiritual heritage, your skills and knowledge. These things have permanent value – which is not measured in dollars and cents.

Waypoint #3: Be Specific.

Finally, don't do this at home. If you're going to make the effort, do it well. Record it digitally with a specific agenda, facilitated by competent counsel.

To learn more about the Waypoints, or to find an estate advisor in your area that practices legacy planning, check out www.garywinterlaw.com/waypoints.

ABOUT GARY

Attorney Gary Winter's business and estate planning practice focuses on helping entrepreneurial families enhance their lives today and secure their futures tomorrow. He excels in guiding his clients through the often confusing maze of financial and legal decisions to create plans that ensure the well-being of their families, businesses and the accomplishment of cherished family goals. His considerable legal expertise includes family and business protection, wealth preservation and values-based planning. Whether you are a startup or established business, with a traditional family or blended family, just starting out or looking back on a life well-lived, Gary will help you craft a plan that achieves your goals for your business and loved ones today and for years to come.

After a ten year career as a commercial airline pilot, Gary graduated second in his law school class from San Joaquin College of Law in 2006 and served as a judicial extern to the Honorable Justice Timothy S. Buckley on the 5th District Court of Appeal in 2005. While at San Joaquin College of Law, Gary received Bernard E. Witkin Academic Excellence Awards for being at the top of the class in Legal Research and Writing, Criminal Law and Legal Remedies. Gary also won the Best Brief award and was a Best Oral Advocate Finalist in the George A. Hopper Moot Court Competition in 2005. Gary was a member of the school's scholarly publication, The San Joaquin Agricultural Law Review, from 2003 to 2006. After graduation, Gary was an associate at the prestigious law firm of McCormick, Barstow, Sheppard, Wayte and Carruth, LLP, where he represented high net-worth families and their businesses, in their real estate, business and estate matters. Before opening his own practice, Gary was a partner with the law firm of Powell and Pool, PC, which specialized in representing lenders.

In 2008, Gary was published as author of a professional article in the Review advocating for farmers' rights to cancel Williamson Act contracts. The article is titled *"Does A Williamson Act Contract Have Constitutional Status?"* (17 SJALR 1 (2008)). Gary advocates for efficient and green use of real estate and has written several articles for websites on the complex subject of fractional ownership of vacation homes, which allows owners to buy, use and sell their proportional fractional (1/6th, 1/8th, etc.) interest in a vacation home. In December, 2008 Gary was featured in "Fractional Properties: Own a Piece of Paradise" in *Where to Retire* magazine. Gary is a frequent lecturer for real estate brokers on the subjects of co-ownership and business planning issues. Gary has chosen to serve entrepreneurial families because he is passionate about helping families create happy and secure futures.

Most importantly, Gary is husband to Julie and proud father of Marci, Lanson and Jackson.

CHAPTER 18

CAN YOU REALLY DO WITHOUT MONEY?

BY ROBERT GALLIANO, ESQ.

More than money does not mean "No money at all".

Security, peace of mind and a future assured for those you leave behind are what you also want to leave. So, how do you achieve all of this?

I had two good friends, Ric and Jeff, and a great client, Molly, I only say 'great' because Molly listened and acted on my advice.

Let me tell you their stories. Ric was a Financial Planner, very successful (Ric really knew his stuff), married with two lovely young children. I first met Ric when we had worked together on a few cases; this business relationship and friendship went on for more than three years. We used to talk a lot about the "when it happens to us", what do we want to leave our family?

Well, obviously we wanted to leave something but what did we really want to leave?

Ah, yes… we wanted to leave our family with the security that they would have enough money to weather whatever storm came their way, enough for the kids to be raised so they would have a good education, and for our spouses to have peace of mind that all debts would be paid. Fair enough.

Ric and I knew that one way to achieve this was with life insurance, and since we both were in the Insurance business we shopped to find the best insurance for the best price. We both promised each other that we would get this insurance no matter what. We found the right company, I applied, but Ric did not. I asked Ric, "Why aren't you applying?"

We both agreed to get insurance. "Do it! It is for your family." …but Ric procrastinated. (Do you know what procrastination is? It is the thief of time.) He gave one excuse after another. You have heard this one, I am sure, …"I am too fat," and "I need to lose weight so I can get a cheaper rate," and so on. Time went by and you guessed it, Ric died suddenly over a weekend. We later found out that Ric, unbeknown to him, had cancer that had metastasized into his lungs and over the weekend his lungs collapsed. Ric died leaving two young children and a young wife, without security and peace of mind. Ric left his family penniless.

Jeff, my other friend, a genius inventor, was working day and night, inventing a computer keyboard that would eliminate Carpal Tunnel Syndrome. Jeff was a young inventor, with a young wife and two small children. … getting the picture? Jeff's motto was: *"Don't tell me not to burn the candle at both ends. Tell me where to get more wax!"*

Jeff was told over and over to think about his family and not just his "keyboard". Jeff was obsessed by getting his "keyboard" into production, spending every penny saved in order to succeed. When we talked about what we would leave our family, if and when we left this earth, Jeff always said "I want to leave them lots of money" and I would ask him why? Jeff would say "So they would have security and peace of mind, not have to worry about the bills," and *"If you think nobody cares, try missing a couple of payments."*

Well, Jeff was so involved, day and night, stressing over his "keyboard" that one morning, his heart literally exploded and Jeff was gone, just like that, and like Ric, left his young wife and two kids penniless.

So here are two friends that died young and unexpectedly – leaving a family without security, peace of mind and hope. Both of them loved their family deeply, but were consumed with work or a need to get the absolute bargain price for something of value. Both ignored the need to plan for the inevitable, and more importantly, to act on it.

Molly on the other hand, had a young husband and two small kids. She listened to and acted upon my advice and purchased a "whopping amount" of insurance. When she was diagnosed with "Lou Gehrig's" disease that consumed her in a matter of months, she left her family well taken care of ... leaving them hope, peace of mind and security.

Hope, peace of mind and security are intangibles, they can't be bought, these are feelings that you either have or you don't, but sometimes "money" can provide you with the framework to be able to achieve that.

I am not saying that you absolutely have to leave your family well off, but "money" can sure help. *"If you die early, life insurance is the best asset you can own. If you die late, it probably isn't the worst asset you can own.*" So why not have some.

I am not trying to sell you on life insurance, but here are a few comments on the subject:

There are many types of insurance. As an example, there is "Term" insurance and "Whole Life" – the kind that builds a cash value over time. I tend to favor "Term" insurance for younger families, particularly for its simplicity. Planning financial goals around a cash value insurance plan can get really complicated. There are non-trivial rules governing things like the size of your cash value savings versus the policy death benefit, and the repayment of policy loans. Term life, on the other hand, is the essence of simplicity -- pay the premium, get covered for the term.

Because they are so simple, term life policies can be easily compared on the basis of price. This has led to a very competitive market in which term life policies are rapidly becoming a commodity. If you go to Google you will find an easy way to compare companies.

Many term policies are both "renewable" and "convertible." The former ensures that you can re-up for another term policy without a medical exam. The latter allows you to convert your term life policy into an equivalent cash value policy from the same carrier, should this make sense during the term of the policy.

Not all term life policies offer these features however, so be sure to ask for them specifically if you want them. (In particular, be sure you know what they mean by "renewable.") On the other hand, cash value policies only work out well when they are held for life. Once you're in, it's tough to get out without a little financial pain. There may be heavy surrender charges that make it tough to walk away.

However, I need to be fair and point out when you may need to consider cash value life insurance policies.

Planning to pay estate taxes is not a big deal to most people, as our estates may be of a modest size ...the federal exemption from estate taxes in 2010 is unlimited, with the current law (at the time of this writing) returning to one million dollars in 2011. Nonetheless, if you are planning to leave a multimillion-dollar pot of gold for your heirs (or you have a long-lost uncle!), and want Uncle Sam's hands kept out of it, you may want to sit down with an estate planning specialist.

Many times when you are approaching your golden years, term insurance will be extremely expensive, and may not be available at all. In this case, cash value life insurance may be the only way to provide your spouse with sufficient replacement income, should you die first and failed to save up a decent 'nest egg'.

So, what is my advice to you? What simple steps can you take so you can leave your family with those precious things – like hope, peace of mind and security?

First, figure out what your family would need if you were to suddenly leave this earth. Calculate the worst conditions, like unexpected debts and illness. Add to this what they would like to accomplish in life, like educational goals, standard of living, things that they would be able to have if you were still around. Most of us always want our kids to have a better life than what we had.... better education, less stress, more freedom to do what they want.

Second, you have to be realistic and determine what you can afford.

Third and most importantly, just do it! You cannot be a Ric or a Jeff. Life can end unexpectedly and you want to be prepared and assured that you are leaving your family "more than money".

Carry enough insurance…you may want to adopt Jack Benny's attitude:

"I don't want to tell you how much insurance I carry with the Prudential, but all I can say is: when I go, they go too."

~ Jack Benny

ABOUT ROBERT

Robert J. Galliano JD, Attorney-at-Law, Certified by the California State Bar as a Specialist in Estate Planning, Trust, and Probate Law practices primarily in the Temecula Valley since he was admitted to the California State Bar in 1981.

Robert has a Bachelor of Science in Electrical Engineering as well as a Master of Science in Taxation. He is a member of the National Academy of Elder Law Attorneys and a Financial Advisor.

This extensive background allows Robert to see what families need to ensure the peace, security, and financial stability that is required when a family member dies.

Robert is a nationally sought-after speaker on what families need so they can have a foolproof plan that will protect their family. Robert has been helping families work toward financial security with his personalized approach to wealth planning, accumulation and preservation. Robert's goal is to help maintain the standard of living his clients have become accustomed to, and to preserve their wealth for their children and grandchildren.

To learn more about Robert Galliano, visit: www.gallianolaw.com, or call (951) 694-3884.